MW00426276

INFINITELY MORE

INFINITELY

MORE

CHOOSING FREEDOM, A CAREER MOM'S TURNING POINT

AMY CONWAY-HATCHER

NEW DEGREE PRESS

COPYRIGHT © 2021 AMY CONWAY-HATCHER
All rights reserved.

INFINITELY MORE
Choosing Freedom, A Career Mom's Turning Point

ISBN   978-1-63730-648-2   *Paperback*
              978-1-63730-731-1   *Kindle Ebook*
              978-1-63730-922-3   *Ebook*

For Olivia and Jack,
May you always dream big, be curious, and stay true to yourselves.
Wherever you go, whatever mountains you climb,
Dad and I love you to the moon and back.

For all those who support, lift up, champion, and sponsor women
and girl warriors of all generations, I am humbled by you.

All proceeds of this book will be donated to Together
Rising, Girl Up, YoungLeaders.World, and the Women's
Bar Association Foundation of Washington, DC.

Contents

Despite her fears she found,
The secret to an outstanding life,
Is risking the fall,
For the possibility of flight.

—KYRA JACKSON

Author's Note

Guess what? Someone solved our problem—why women aren't getting ahead, my friend said, her voice dripping with sarcasm.

It's because when women become moms, we lose focus and don't work hard enough.

My friend burst out laughing. *Thank goodness we know. We just have to work harder. . . .*

Are you kidding? Someone actually said that—again? I said, stunned.

Frustrated, I thought, it's no wonder women leave their jobs. Leaders don't really care about the stories behind the surveys. Women also get terrible advice.

I wondered if it was possible for us to get smarter—about seeing system inequities, pushing for change, and choosing differently. I was intrigued if there was a way to make leaders see reality. And, if not, whether women could use this moment to change the game we play.

FACING HARD REALITIES AND A DIFFICULT CHOICE: SPEAK OUT OR STAY SILENT?

It had been five months since I left my high-paying equity partner job in Big Law, my third law firm. A month after my friend's phone call.

I was still stewing.

Not about my exit. About the age-old debate and hand-wringing over the advancement and retention of women in the workforce.

Women were leaving jobs, and it seemed like we were back to the same old song.

Men were sitting around their tables dumbfounded, sounding alarms about retaining women and the lack of women at their table.

Women were lamenting progress lost. Yet, we also were going down that endless path of wondering if we'd achieved, climbed, sacrificed, or worked hard enough.

Organizations and leaders were "doubling down" on diversity—again. Or was it the fourth or eighty-second time? I can't remember. It's not important.

What is important is that *this time* everyone was really, fully, truly, and completely *recommitted* to *doubling down* on the problem of keeping women at work and in conference room chairs.

I wasn't buying it. I was still recovering from shoulder surgery and my soul-crushing burnout experience.

From working too hard in my pressure-cooker job.

Where I spent countless days, nights, and weekends away from my life and family for over two decades to deliver millions in revenue for the benefit of my partners.

In a male-dominated environment that was neither equal nor fair.

That required more of me than my male peers.

This was around the same time a woman career coach penned an article offering her two cents on what women must do to advance. Sounding eerily like the "work harder" advice I received from women leaders who came before me, I bristled.

The article set off a firestorm of responses online. Women offered proof they were pulling off herculean feats every day. To be perceived as excellent in every way. To meet warped expectations as they juggled a million balls in the air.

They were doing the climb like I did. To rise above barriers and uneven playing fields. To achieve success they dreamed of and no doubt deserved.

My heart wept for them. I wanted to tell them to stop and save themselves. The climb was worse than they thought, especially as you got to the upper echelons.

PUTTING MY TOE IN THE WATER, FACING A STARK REALIZATION

At the urging of friends, I wrote an article rejecting the "work harder," "do more" position (Conway-Hatcher 2021).

I argued that women have exceeded our end of the deal to meet lofty workplace expectations. If the workplace wanted us to stay, it was time for the unequal system to change. Otherwise, it was a bad one-sided exchange for women. I was proof the "work harder," "do more" advice didn't work.

Then came the avalanche of responses and private messages from women across industries, especially Big Law.

Women agreed with my argument, but many shared privately they felt muzzled. So long as they're in the system they can't say what's wrong with it.

That's right, despite our progress, women still don't feel free to speak up about systemic workplace inequities that continue to hold us back.

Even in my own profession, the legal industry, where the core of our day jobs requires us to advocate for justice and the fair treatment of our clients, yet we can't speak up for ourselves at home base.

I didn't blame women for feeling this way.

They were right. It's impossible to say what you think when you're in the system.

Men don't want to hear it. Women don't want to say it.

Women must walk a fine line. We don't want to be viewed as complainers, nor labeled as bitchy, ungrateful, or demanding. We want to be seen as team players and avoid retribution or punishment for speaking the truth.

But here's the problem.

If women can't call out inequities, how can we expect anything to change? And what does it say about the broader system if women lawyers, the same ones who seek justice for others, must remain mute for themselves?

Frustrated, I wanted to say out loud:

> *When is someone going to share real stories about why women leave big jobs or professions—the gritty, messy stories behind the surveys . . . the kind no one wants to hear or acknowledge or see—so that we can finally stop doing the same things that don't work? So that we can find better strategies ahead?*

In the silence that followed, I had to face my own truth: that, despite being known as a straight-shooter in my work with clients—the one who "calls it like it is"—I couldn't speak openly about problems in my own organizations or industry, or at least I got tired of trying. Speaking into the abyss wasn't very satisfying or encouraging.

But I knew the truth, as uncomfortable and annoying as it might feel. We must be willing to talk about what's wrong if we ever hope to get it right.

After ruminating about it, I summoned the courage to make a call to my editor, a call that changed everything.

Hi Regina, It's me. I'm ready to write that book I swore I'd never write.

WHY WOMEN LEAVE BIG JOBS

Yes, women are leaving their jobs. The data proves it.

"Women in the Workplace 2020," a study by McKinsey & Company and LeanIn.org, said one in four women were considering changing their careers or leaving the workforce. It impacted millions of women workers, potentially erasing decades of gender diversity progress.

Reports for my industry of Big Law reflected losses too. In 2021, Law360 and the American Bar Association reported only nominal gains in the advancement of women lawyers and a steady flow of women leaving law firms, including at the senior ranks. Men and women weren't even on the same page about gender issues.

Yet, while parts of the surveys resonated with me, they didn't (and couldn't) really explain why women leave their jobs nor why I left mine. It wasn't childcare or burnout from the pandemic. It was far more complicated than that:

> An even harsher picture of the workforce exposing a more troubling side of systems still not designed to support and champion highly talented, skilled, and qualified women to rise to the tops of organizations—and stay there.

> The layers of wounds and harm done when women play uneven games we were never intended to win.

> The potential impact for future generations if we fail to break the cycle now.

Looking back at my twenty-eight-year career, first as a prosecutor of violent crimes, and then as a Big Law defender of corporations, I realized that if I ran into a brick wall, just about anyone could.

I thought I was doing everything right. Competing on merit. Playing the uneven game I was offered. Looking back now, I can see where I played that game well. Yet, I also see tactical errors and perhaps where I failed to accept what I was truly up against.

THE TRUTH

On March 8, 2021, International Women's Day, I announced my decision to leave Big Law.

I attributed it to a family decision and my choice to take on a lighter schedule. While true, it didn't give the full picture nor the real challenges and tensions that finally took their toll.

I didn't think anyone would care.

The truth is I made the decision to leave Big Law because I lost faith in the system I'd served and accommodated for more than twenty years. A system that treated me differently than my male peers in very significant ways, and yet was indifferent to the extraordinary strain it places on women, especially as women rise into the upper levels.

> From whopping compensation differences, to lack of leadership opportunities, to additional administrative burdens, these environments were rife with biases and interactions that were infinitely less welcoming, friendly, and supportive of women.

> Then, there were extra, time-consuming tasks women take on to make others "feel" better or more comfortable about being in the presence of a strong woman—tasks that make our jobs infinitely harder.

> And, of course, we took on flag-waving roles to support minimally funded diversity programs that had no chance of success. It's a "ruse" men and women perpetuated for different reasons that allows the system to continue in exactly the way it was intended. The *haves* stay in control. The *have nots* play on the second-string teams.

Weary and discouraged from competing on a field where no one expected me to win, I talked with my kids, Olivia and Jack, and my husband, Sid.

They were done with my ridiculous schedule and the frustrations I brought home about an industry that had become more about money than people, an industry that wasn't honest about the barriers and challenges women face at work every day—from systemic barriers and biases to the demeaning and boorish.

A CROSSROADS AND AN IMPORTANT CHOICE

The exodus of women puts us at a crossroads of choosing to continue the same cycle or to create new possibilities.

I wrote *Infinitely More* to offer insights into the "real deal" of why women leave big jobs, and how leaders lose them, through the lens of my own story, journey, and realizations.

You'll see stories of key events in my early life and career that shaped my approach and attitude toward my Big Law climb, how I navigated through a historically male-dominated world. You'll read gritty anecdotes that offer a window into the reality of life for women on these professional battlefields.

You won't find sugar coating or artificial sweeteners, but you will see glimmers of possibilities—callouts of important lessons learned, reflections, and thoughts on how we might tackle the road ahead.

The book is intended to show the raw emotion, blood, sweat, and tears women experience climbing through hierarchies of organizations, especially Big Law:

What life looks like when women start their careers and sign up to make the climb. Our hopes, dreams, and ambitions.

The trade-offs and bargains we strike along the way to meet expectations.

The fairytales we tell ourselves to keep going and stay on track.

The tough lessons, sad truths, and hard realities we face or rationalize away.

The choices we're forced to make when faced with our own crossroads.

The silver linings we find through lessons learned, our own empowerment, and perhaps better strategies for the future.

I dive into the heart of my personal stories to demonstrate the great responsibilities and heavy burdens we women carry no matter what job we have.

We shoulder our own dreams and the hopes of the next generation with the expectations of the generation before. We wave diversity flags to support our sisters and tiptoe around tough issues to make things more comfortable for our husbands, brothers, fathers, and colleagues. On any given day, we do our level-headed best not to disappoint our mothers while blazing paths for our children.

We stand together. We stand alone.

MY HOPE AND DREAM FOR THIS BOOK

Like any author and type A woman, I've fretted about the risk of this book. If it does nothing more than entertain you with humorous and enlightening stories about the rise, battles, redemption, and relaunching of a career mom whose kids and unexpected heroes wouldn't let her off the hook, I can accept that.

I do hope for more. After all, the exodus of women didn't just happen. I hope it rings like the piercing alarm bell it is.

My dream for this book is about possibilities and helping each of us believe in and protect our power to choose.

I hope that by speaking out and sharing my story, I will encourage and empower you to reflect on your own journey, to decide for yourself—with eyes wide open—whether the trade-offs you make within the system you serve are worth the price you are paying. And, if not, that you can speak out, change your career strategy, or seek new possibilities instead.

I hope that leaders and our male colleagues lean in, listen closely, and for once, take the bolder, intentional steps needed to even out woefully imbalanced playing fields. Not just at lower levels where garnering support is easier, but through to the upper echelons where imbalances are even more striking and play a significant role in whether senior women decide to stay.

I hope that what starts out as one woman's whisper and wish to the universe begins a renewed conversation free of bullshit and half-truths. Free of platitudes and hugs. Free of fake cheers and flags. Free of greasy poles, barriers, and uneven burdens.

And last but not least,

I hope that women find the courage to play a new game that fundamentally changes the playing field and the conversation for future generations so that our daughters and granddaughters realize even more opportunities ahead.

That's right.

My big dream is that we begin to take *actual* steps toward equality and unlimited opportunities for willing, talented, hard-working women.

After all, we're worth it—and infinitely more.

It's a unicorn dream I know.

But what else should you do with a dream?

You live it and, with any luck, you change the world.

You are allowed to be both a masterpiece
and a work in progress simultaneously.

—SOPHIA BUSH

PART I
THE GIRL WARRIOR

Owning our story can be hard but not nearly as difficult as spending our lives running from it.

—BRENÉ BROWN

If people are doubting how far you can go, go so far that you can't hear them anymore.

—MICHELE RUIZ

Ode to Burnout

I don't know exactly how it happened or even when it started. The monster called Burnout had been stalking me for years.

Lurking. Leering. Hovering.

I knew she was there. I felt her. I feared her.

But I didn't listen. I did what I thought any self-respecting career woman in the rough and tumble corporate world would do.

I pretended she was nothing. I shunned her. I gave her no power, no voice, no identity, no measure of importance. I let her fester. There was no room in my wildly busy, successful life.

Looking back, I realize that in my silence, insolence, pride, and irreverence, I provoked her.

To those who say "Hell hath no fury like a woman scorned," you haven't met Burnout.

She could give that lady a run for her money—any day.

Burnout is as soul-crushing, demoralizing, and physically drain-ing as anything you could imagine.

I know. I've met her.

CHAPTER 1

My Kitchen Meltdown

It was a cold winter day in January 2021. Lying in bed, I watched the sunlight flicker through a window in a lame attempt to distract myself. The pain from shoulder surgery was searing, worse than childbirth. It felt like someone took a steel bat to my right shoulder before piercing it with a carving knife deep in the socket, twisting it for good measure. Muscle spasms that seized my arm and back didn't help. By week four, sleep was elusive, tears frequent, sadness consuming. Weak, broken, empty, I had nothing left to give.

Wincing, I hauled my body from bed to get pain medicine and a cup of tea. I chastised myself. *How could I have been so stupid?*

A ridiculous home accident. A distracted working mom. My mind was used to churning at warp speed like a high-functioning command center. I never focused on one thing. But when my foot caught my pant leg, it was over in an instant. I had no time to react. Picture a ripe melon slamming onto a hardwood floor at full force. That was my shoulder.

The surgeon laughed. *You need a better story given what you do,* he said, *like tackling a burglar.* Point taken.

Twenty minutes later, I sat in my kitchen watching steam drift off my tea, waiting for the medicine to kick in. I wondered how long before I could get back to "normal" life.

Yet, strangely, I had to admit the forced break from my insane work schedule was a relief. No marathon conference calls. No midnight drafting sessions. No 3:00 a.m. wake-up alarms to wade through a tsunami of unread emails. No Big Law bean-counter sending me time-sheet reminders (those daily reports law firms use to track every task that can be billed to a client in six-minute increments).

I was exhausted; not in the usual battle-worn, working mom kind of way; not from the surgery. This went deeper. The pace of my life—the never-ending demands and the lack of support in my job despite high expectations—finally seemed to be catching up with me.

Some friends suggested I change law firms again. The job market was hot for women with my experience and track record. Their firms were hiring.

You could easily increase your salary, I'd been told. It was tempting. My brain whirled. I wasn't sure I was up for a fourth firm. I had some decisions to make.

Hi Mom, can we talk? Lost in my thinking fog, I hadn't noticed my twelve-year-old son Jack walk into the kitchen. Something was on his mind.

Dad told me you might have another opportunity. He said it's a lot of money. Soooo, um, how much are we talking about?

I tried not to laugh. Leave it to Jack to pull me back to Earth.

You're funny. None of your business on the money. But it sounds like you have questions?

Yes, I have questions, he said shuffling his feet, *and I have some concerns.*

Pulling up a stool, Jack looked more serious. He took a slow, deep breath. He met my gaze. Then, he rattled off a series of questions.

Was it the same kind of job? Would it require as much travel? Would I be on my phone all the time? Would I be able to pick him up at school? Would I watch his volleyball games in person? Would I still work vacations? Would I be around for family dinners?

With each question, my chest tightened. I had no idea where this was going. It was like a cross between *Double Jeopardy* and the lightening round of *Family Feud.*

Jack paused. Another deep breath as his eyes welled up.

Mom, he said softly, *I think it's important for you to pursue opportunities, especially when it's a lot of money. We know you have to work hard in your job—but, this time, can you tell that law firm I want my mom? Olivia and I need you too.*

Returning my son's bearhug with my good arm, I promised I would think about everything he said. A short time later, he let go and left the room.

As he turned the corner, I wept.

A WARRIOR CAREER MOM

I don't cry often. I don't have time. I am a warrior career mom. If a cry is needed, it has to fit in the schedule. Otherwise, it must wait.

In my career, I am one of those lawyers no one ever wants to *need*—a keeper of secrets, solver of mysteries, and fierce advocate. Clients hire me to keep them out of trouble, protect their good names, and solve the kind of legal problems no one wants you to know about.

Some wonder if my "high-powered" job is like one of those badass Washington, DC television drama series, like *Scandal*. The job is intense but not quite that dramatic. We don't hack into government systems, torture people, or consort with leaders of the free world. That said, we see some pretty crazy stuff, including the kind of corporate or political scandals you read about in the papers.

Many of us are former federal prosecutors who left government service to reap the financial rewards of private practice. Our work requires the meticulous analysis of evidence—like emails, witness interviews, and financial data. We track breadcrumbs, evaluate theories, find puzzle pieces. We think about what makes people tick, their motives, their endgames, and how to maneuver among our adversaries. The strategic chess board can consume my brain, especially late at night when the phone isn't demanding my attention.

At home, I am the mom of two amazing kids and wife of a retired naval officer and helicopter test pilot. As a career mom, I do whatever is needed to spend "quality" time with my family and keep the trains running. Over time, I've learned to accept this includes both visible and invisible tasks that may not be universally understood, and that women shoulder more often than men.

Here's just a glimpse of what I might put on a "mom" resume.

> I'm the master of schedules and planner of vacations, birthday parties, holidays, camps, sports, music lessons, doctor appointments, and caretakers. I am a giver of unconditional love, hugs, kisses, and praise. I manage the daily crises of forgotten lunch bags, skinned knees, missed homework, sneakers that don't fit, teen drama, stomach aches, and sore throats. If needed, I am the traffic cop and even the jailer when attitudes need correcting. I do the regular house stuff too. I'm far from perfect, but I do my best to be there for my kids even if it means sacrificing what little sleep I get.

I could go on, but you get the picture. Like my career job, the mom gig is 24/7.

BEHIND THE FAÇADE

For years, I prided myself on being one of those career moms who seemingly "did it all." An equity partner in Big Law at her peak earning years, I reached the milestone of a seven-figure salary years ago. Expectations for the job were high, but my cases were money-makers. Leaders seemed to love the work I was doing. They'd pat my shoulder in the elevator or leave me a year-end voicemail at compensation time. They said I had a seat at the table.

While some days were an utter disaster, most probably seemed unremarkable to those who weren't in the thick of a case with me. I seemed to move effortlessly between battlefields and playgrounds, courtrooms and classrooms, prosecutors and playdates, international air travel and carpool, birthday cupcakes and boardroom dinners.

You never saw me sweat. You rarely heard me worry. You never knew how many balls I could effortlessly juggle in the air.

Well—not really. The effortless part was all bullshit. I guess it's what I told myself to survive. Or perhaps it was what I wanted the world to see. Or maybe it was what I thought the world expected of someone like me.

I knew how darn lucky I was to make it this far. I was "a success story," among the small percentage of women to play among the big boys. On hard days, I'd remind myself: *Hang in there. Keep your head up. Other people have it worse.*

Women like me who make it this far are supposed to be grateful to have a place on the team, a seat at the proverbial "table," whatever that is. We aren't supposed to complain or show weakness. We aren't supposed to take our foot off the gas or say when we've had enough. We are expected to soldier on in the climb.

Do more. Be more. Win more. Love more. Fight more. Endure more.

Yet, what no one really says is this: The climb is more like a death-defying high-wire juggling act on a razor-thin rope over a cliff.

I'll admit it. I love a good competition. I'm energized by the thrill of playing tough games. Not only do I thrive in that environment, I'm also quite good at it. This Big Law career mom pace, however, became inhumane and unsustainable— even for a tough, competitive, resourceful gal like me.

Yet, I still thought if I got a seat at the power table, perhaps I could change things. I could help them see what was actually happening to women like me. Yes, I'm talking about the *real table*, not the table that looked a bit like the rickety kids' table at my grandmother's Thanksgiving dinner.

Getting to that real table, though, proved tougher than I imagined. Despite my success, there were challenges I didn't foresee. Goal posts kept moving. Business priorities kept shifting. Aspirations kept changing. What was touted as true during the job recruiting phase about a law firm's strategies or support for career women wasn't always reality when you got behind the curtain. In fact, for many women, Big Law reality was far different.

Much like my grandmother's house at Thanksgiving, you didn't move up to the real table unless someone died—or left the family for good—or you happened to be a favored child who was given a special turn.

Egos loomed large. The family culture ruled. To be among the inner circle, you had to wait your turn.

Even then, there's a pecking order that changes depending on who's in favor.

By early 2021, I had run out of gas. I wasn't alone.

A PREDICTABLE EXODUS OF WOMEN

When I read the McKinsey & Company and LeanIn.org study, "Women in the Work Place 2020," I wasn't surprised. The problem was I didn't buy what some were saying—that the pandemic was the source of the problem. It may have been the straw that broke the camel's back, but it wasn't the root cause.

Pinning it on the pandemic seemed like a copout. It could let leaders off the hook too easily.

While every woman's story is unique, and there may be women who were going strong, the truth is many women were burning out before 2020 (Meredith Corporation, 2019). I know, I was one of them. What really made me mad was that everyone knew it. There were studies, articles, and research. As leadership teams sat at their tables now wringing their hands, I feared another faux diversity plan.

The cynical voice in my head said they didn't get it. Worse, I wasn't entirely sure anyone wanted to. It seemed easier, perhaps more convenient for them to overlook and oversimplify serious, complex, and continuing problems for women in the workplace. I felt like I'd been dealing with that for years.

The more I thought about my own journey and experience, the worse I felt.

In more than twenty years of Big Law practice, it was a rare occurrence that any Big Law leader asked what it was like to be a woman making the climb in law firm and client environments that, in many cases, were male-dominated. Nor did they ask what it took to juggle complex cases, clients, kids, family, and never-ending firm demands—or even systemic biases I faced in the workplace.

Part of the problem is that most leaders have no clue about the challenges women face in the organizations they lead. Neatly packaged surveys or summary reports only tell you so much. And so they continue to fail to appreciate the many burdens women carry, seen and unseen, at work and home.

When it comes to retaining women or understanding why women leave, leaders have no idea what challenges need to be addressed.

THE VIEW FROM THE BURNOUT DITCH

Thirty years ago, I came to Washington, DC a determined, tough, resourceful girl intent on changing the world.

She was not a quitter, I thought, smiling to myself in my kitchen. She was resilient. She had grit in spades. Nothing seemed impossible.

As a prosecutor, the younger version of me put bad guys in jail. Like that guy who grabbed a young girl on her way to school and raped her in an abandoned building. Or the guy who strangled his grandmother with his bare hands. Or the gang member who murdered his rivals.

As a defense attorney, that same girl traveled the world investigating fraud, international bribery, and trails of money. She stared down government agents, maneuvered through C-suites, and challenged adversaries.

Somewhere along the line, I lost that girl full of grit. I wondered where she went. What tempered her spirit?

I had been working insane Big Law hours under incredibly stressful conditions for a long time. My job is action packed. On top of the work itself, people in crisis need a lot of handholding, especially tough leaders who are used to being in charge.

Back at home, I was juggling middle-school kids facing rough middle-school struggles. Like many Gen Xers, I also began facing unexpected emergencies with aging parents. This was all on top of the myriad responsibilities of being a Big Law partner in a competitive, cutthroat environment.

Yet, as law firm leaders sat at their table celebrating my successes and hours logged in recent years, I was struggling. Hanging on by my fingernails.

To experience burnout for a career warrior mom like me didn't happen overnight. When I hit the wall, it was soul-crushing. To admit it to anyone, unfathomable. I felt inadequate, depressed, anxious, unappreciated, alone, and powerless.

Once impenetrable, the layers of my warrior suit were in tatters—shredded like thin layers of fabric. There was nothing to protect me. I couldn't breathe.

As the tears fell softly on my face on that cold winter day after my chat with Jack, I began questioning everything from my career to motherhood. In typical chick fashion, I blamed myself.

- How could a warrior career mom—*a superhero*—turn into such a pitiful, weak version of her former self? How could I have lost my sense of mission and purpose?

- Was I a terrible mother? How had I miscalculated the needs of my kids? Did I screw up their childhood by not being around more?

- Was the price tag of "success" worth it? Does any warrior career mom ever come out unscathed?

Despite major career wins, I wasn't sure if my work mattered or, worse, if I mattered. I felt like a widget representing a bucket of hours. Nothing more. Nothing less.

PEELING BACK THE ONION

Crap, I thought, my mind racing as I stared out the window of my kitchen stirring my tea. *Maybe Gary Heil was right.*

Gary is an expert and award-winning author I'd been consulting on my leadership research for a book I'd been writing during the pandemic. I thought it might help me understand the flaws in leadership I'd been seeing in my industry and the world. I challenged Gary to explain why the leadership industry was producing such crummy leaders. I challenged him on why industry leaders couldn't see what Big Law had become? Where was the mission and comradery? How could they not see the extraordinary challenges women continued to face?

Much to my chagrin, Gary had me pegged. On the one hand, I wanted to believe I could buck the system, overcome the odds, achieve great things, and make the world better. On the other hand, I was stuck on a hamster wheel, running the same race, frustrated with my rickety cage but unable to eject. I was desperate for change, yet I clung to the familiar.

Maybe it isn't just the leaders? The research shows that people like predictability, even when it isn't good for them, Gary was fond of saying. *We don't think we run with the herd, but we do.*

Time and again, Gary turned my arguments around on me. I was blaming the leaders, and maybe that was partly right.

But what about me? What about cultures that are hard to change? My career environment was insane, inequitable, and the climb unsustainable, yet I stayed. Like all humans, perhaps I was more comfortable in a predictable system than out of it.

And then, there was the money, the chain that bound me to the hamster wheel. How was I any different than the leaders?

Of course, my first reaction was to stubbornly fight Gary's ideas. After one of our spirited debates, I stomped around the house much to the amusement of my family.

I can't believe he said that. I don't run with a herd! I am not part of the Big Law problem. I have no problem bucking the system!

That's when the family reminded me of "the Bitch story." *Maybe it's not simple after all,* they said, making me question myself.

I *hate* it when they do that.

"THE BITCH STORY"

One late afternoon, I called a well-respected senior male partner and lifer at my then-firm seeking advice. I was leading a team on a tough matter for a client he knew well. As is common in these crises, the client was under pressure and highly stressed. I'm used to that norm. But one client lawyer was treating people poorly, undermining the team, and making risky decisions that weren't vetted—which, in our cases, can lead to disaster. Everyone was working 24/7. I hoped my partner and the firm could help.

After listening for a few minutes, my partner sighed. He was aware of the issues. He agreed we were in a tough situation. He didn't envy me. He was glad he wasn't in my shoes. But this was an important firm client. No one was willing to rock the boat. For better or worse, I needed to accept that I was the client's bitch. I had to manage whatever they threw at me.

Protect the team the best you can, he said wishing me luck. I held the phone stunned.

MY CROSSROADS

I remembered sharing the "bitch story" with my kids. Horrified, Olivia couldn't believe that her warrior mom took that from anyone. Frankly, I couldn't either.

I shook my head at the memory. It reminded me of how shocked I was that I'd reached a point of mattering so little to a profession and industry to which I'd devoted so much.

That's when I realized I had some work to do. It was time to understand how that determined, tough, resourceful girl who came to Washington to change the world wound up chained to a hamster wheel.

Deciding to go down this path and open Pandora's Box wasn't easy.

I was afraid where this might lead. It was easy to pin everything on nameless, faceless Big Law, but there were other realities I'd have to confront. Like what role I may have played that didn't help. Where I had accommodated the unequal system. Or ignored things I shouldn't have. Or the roles played by peers, friends, or leaders, whom I liked.

It's like we all pretended the brick wall for women wasn't *really* a brick wall. You know, the brick wall that was always there but covered up in faux paint to look inviting, a more convenient visual. You realize part of what you've dedicated your precious time to was making others feel good about intentional lack of progress—like a trick mirror.

If I spoke, this book would call out some uncomfortable truths and realities that no one likes to acknowledge or talk about. Like all women, I worried what people would think. I don't like being judged or criticized, which is why I started out by writing a comfortable leadership book and, when pressed by the book people and leadership experts, it's why

I stubbornly said I would never write this book or even some of the topics in it. I didn't think I had the guts to say out loud what my friends and I—in and out of Big Law—have talked about for years.

Yet, when I reached a crossroads, I was forced to live the true essence of leadership and who I am deep down. I realized I couldn't complain about a system not changing or others for not speaking out or being courageous if I was unwilling to do that myself, especially if I was truly committed to helping other women reach milestones I didn't. To making their climb easier than mine. Or sharing perspectives so that women didn't fall into the same traps that led me to meeting Burnout.

The hardest part for me, in the end, was knowing that I would have to look in the mirror and judge myself. When all was said and done, would I like what I saw? Would I have regrets? Would the reflection make me weaker or stronger? Would it be worth taking a risk to find out?

That part would take the most courage.

For that, I would need to revive the girl full of grit. She wasn't anyone's bitch.

CHAPTER 2

The Girl Who Came to Washington

In 1990, I arrived in Washington, DC for law school full of idealism and energy. A dreamer of possibilities. I was determined to make a difference in the world.

How? I wasn't sure. I figured my pathway would reveal itself in time. Perhaps when I got a job.

As best I can remember, all first-year law school students had an obligatory meeting with a law school career counsellor. With only three years of law school, there wasn't much time. Most students try to grab permanent jobs by the summer of their second year. Job hunting, like school, was highly competitive.

I was a ball of stress. I had a big problem. Well, more than one.

Washington, DC is like a small town on steroids. It wasn't hard to figure out from the cocky banter among students in between classes that I was an outsider and at a huge deficit.

The polar opposite of "connected." I had no names to drop. No one to open doors. No summer internships on Capitol Hill.

Worse, I wasn't from an elite college nor among the top echelon in ranking. While I had always done well in school, there was no "magna" before the "cum laude." My job history showed grit and financial responsibility, not pedigree.

Resourceful, smart, practical, and determined? There was no doubt. Unfortunately, I was no longer sure *that* was enough.

Walking to the recruiting office from the metro station in the rain, I had a bad feeling. For some reason, I knew the meeting would be deflating. I steeled myself for what was to come.

My radar detected trouble.

After a brief introduction and handshake, the career counsellor invited me to sit in an uncomfortable plastic chair at a round table. It was a bad omen. I hate plastic chairs.

As she began to talk, I could tell she wasn't invested. Our approach to this job hunt of mine couldn't be more different. I was focused on finding a job that mattered and invested countless hours researching potential options that piqued my interest. The career counsellor's goal was to help me find "a job." Nothing more. Nothing less. Her bored expression made it clear: *This kid from New England was a less exciting candidate.*

After listening to my career goals for a few minutes, she asked for my list of job targets, extending her hand. In that moment, I had a quick chat with myself. *Okay, give her the list of jobs if that's what she wants. But don't listen to a word she says. Go for your Plan A.* I knew what was coming.

She paused for what seemed like an eternity as she scanned my list. I couldn't help noticing the faint grimace. Her eyebrows arched. Pursed lips. Then, a brief stare into space, pausing as she seemed to try to find words to soften the blow.

Here it comes . . .

> *I appreciate your drive. I'm not trying to discourage you,* she finally said dryly, *but these jobs typically go to the top 10 percent of the class. Even then, sometimes you have to 'know someone.' Have you thought about a Plan B?*

Handing me a preprinted list of her own, she didn't even bother to ask if I knew anyone. I guess it was obvious.

Her list? Depressing. Mediocre. Boring. Nothing remotely close to resembling a "change the world" job. I think I tuned out the rest of what she had to say.

Walking out of the meeting, I was indignant and more than a little pissed. Even knowing I would get my fair share of rejections by aiming high, I decided to reject her lame Plan B. It wasn't even close to my Plan F. I threw her list in the trash can. It felt weirdly exciting. Clearly, I had to work on my pitch. She didn't even try to take me seriously.

Yes. My goals were lofty. But, why not? I was just getting started. As my mom would say:

Why not shoot for the moon? You might as well do what you love.

All I needed was a chance.

I've always hated any insinuation that I wasn't good enough or that I couldn't achieve something—*especially if it came from a woman.* First, I didn't believe it. Second, it wasn't polite. Third, what the heck is sisterhood good for if our first instinct is to squash each other's dreams?

At this point, you might be asking yourself whether, at that time, I thought being a girl would hinder my ability to get a job or keep a job? The answer is NO. Not once.

I was aware of my gender, of course. I knew women were outnumbered in the workplace and that many of the higher ups were men. None of that mattered to me. In my twenties, I was more worried about being young and inexperienced than being a girl.

I believed that girls could do or be anything. It was part of my DNA and preprogrammed long before I came to Washington.

A FAMILY OF WARRIOR WOMEN

I come from a family of strong women warriors. Ahead of their time, my mother and grandmothers had careers and made their own money. My grandmothers worked for a railroad and a hospital. My mom was a surgical nurse, followed by teacher, artist, lawyer, and award-winning photographer.

In our world, there was nothing a girl couldn't do. Or, at least, nothing we would ever admit. Barriers were limits you set in your mind.

Others may have it easier to start, my mom would tell me and my siblings. *But you'll go farther when you prove you belong.*

My mom was a doer. We tried everything as kids.

Express an interest in the moon? We'd find ourselves in a space museum.

Pick up an instrument? We'd wind up in a summer band.

Love a vegetable? We'd discover it planted in the garden.

Like a sport? We'd get a list of local team tryout schedules.

Make it a habit of arguing with your parents? We'd find ourselves in debate camp.

At least you'll be able to structure your arguments more eloquently, my mom would say. Not surprisingly, I attended more than one of those camps.

I have two sisters and a brother. I am the middle girl, the second born. My father still fondly refers to me as #2. There were no girls' or boys' jobs. Just jobs. Everyone was expected to pitch in with equal opportunity, whether we were digging trenches in the mud, bailing water from a flooded basement, tarring the driveway, or cooking dinner.

One evening, when our younger brother was around seven years old, everyone was cleaning up after dinner. Tired and cranky, my brother mistakenly muttered that washing dishes was "a girls' job." The room went still. Deadly silent. Trying not to giggle, my teen sisters and I *almost* felt sorry for him. *Poor little guy,* we whispered.

The blood drained from his face. How he desperately wished he could suck those words out of the air and swallow them whole before they reached our mother's ears. Sadly, it was not to be. After suffering two weeks of kitchen duty under Mom's watchful eye, it was the last time he uttered something so silly. My brother still does the dishes and instills the same values in his sons. He was trained by the best.

In our family, pitching in and working hard was always part of the picture, an expectation but also a privilege. We live in a country where girls can do anything. Opportunities must not be squandered. Whether we were talking school, sports, a job, or a dream, if you fell short of a goal, excuses were pointless. No one else was to blame. No one else would fix it. You had to look at your own effort, recalibrate, and try again.

My parents supported any effort. But your success? That was up to you.

Working hard may sound like a bit of a drag. At times, it was. We're all still scarred from tarring the driveway. I won't even touch that stuff today. But when it came to thinking about future careers? I assure you this mindset was empowering. We owned our destiny. We got to choose. There were no limits.

Dreaming big was embraced. In fact, it was encouraged—so long as the dream didn't begin and end with marrying someone with money. Getting an education and being certain you could support yourself had to be part of the plan. My mom saw too many peers with marriages that crumbled after the kids were grown. Some were forced to get jobs never having worked before. On this topic, she joked, *You never know when your husband might hit his head on a rock and decide to marry a younger version of you.* Of course, my dad knew better than to argue with her.

My dad's career was more traditional, a salesman first and then a stockbroker. My mom was an example of doing something you love for as long as it serves you. She thrived on breaking stereotypes, walking through barriers. She was a good negotiator. Yet, she was not afraid to walk away if the terms weren't fair or if it took her away from what was most important to her at home. Looking back, I still don't know how she did it all. She seemed to have a secret power source that fueled her when most mere mortals needed to rest.

This was my early stomping ground. The foundation upon which my attitude toward jobs and my career was built.

THE KEY THAT OPENED THE DOOR

Every time I think about that law school counsellor, I am grateful to her.

Her flip rejection of my dreams forced me to double down on my job search. My resume didn't suck, but she drove home some important points. I was no longer in a small town. I wasn't from the home team. It was up to me to figure out how to stand out.

Her rejection made me pay closer attention to how I approached each opportunity. It made me rely on what mattered most: My upbringing, my ideals, and my parents' advice permanently etched in my brain.

Work hard. Prove your value.
Make your opportunities. Aim high.
You are responsible for you.

My big chance came when I interviewed for a law clerk position with the Office of International Affairs at the Department of Justice (DOJ). I had passed my resume to the brother of a close college friend, hoping he would take pity on me and give me some pointers. I didn't expect much.

When I got the call, I assumed it was a courtesy. After all, this was an office that handled extraditions and foreign evidence gathering for major international crimes, like: the car bomb explosion that killed diplomat Orlando Letelier on DuPont Circle in 1976, crimes connected to drug lords like Pablo Escobar, or the murder of DEA agent Enrique Camarena by a Mexican cartel in 1985.

It's funny. When you don't expect anything other than a rejection to add to your growing pile of rejections, you feel freer. More authentic. It was a chance to hone my new pitch.

Walking through the formal lobby of a nondescript government building, I remember riding the elevator to a floor with plain, dreary offices and stale carpet. It didn't look like anything special, but it was. I remember feeling important, or at least imagining the potential to feel important. With butterflies in my stomach, I stood straighter.

Among my interviewers that day were two key decision-makers, both women, Lystra, an accomplished lawyer, and the office's long-time senior law clerk.

While the precise words escape me so many years later, the pitch went something like this.

I know you have a lot of people who want this job. I can tell you for sure that I want it more. My goal is to learn. No task is too small or too big. I will take ownership of any assignment, and I welcome feedback. Most importantly, I will work hard. You have an important job. My job is to make your life easier. If you give me a shot, you will never be sorry you hired me.

Instead of talking about what I wanted, I focused on what they needed. I figured who wouldn't want someone whose mission is to make their life easier? I meant every word.

Stunned but thrilled with my job offer, the real work began. I had to prove I belonged.

Juggling school and work was tough. I was all-in. I didn't wait to be asked to help. I showed up early and stayed late. Every assignment—big or small—got my full attention. Whether the case was high profile like Escobar cronies, or seemingly invisible, like the murder of a poor woman abused in El Salvador, the human stories captivated me. Many were difficult to absorb because they were awful and so very different from the world I knew.

As it turns out, my first real legal job ignited something special. I fell in love with the work. Lystra took me under her wing and treated me like a kid sister. She was free with career advice and feedback. She made clear when I had more work to do and celebrated when I nailed it. She shared me with other lawyers to get experience. She looked out for me when it mattered.

A year later, Lystra recommended me for a job in the Organized Crime and Racketeering Section. If I wanted a shot at a permanent DOJ job, she said, I needed to get more experience, work for more people. I hated leaving but was grateful she saw me having the kind of potential worth promoting.

My last two years of law school were a blur, but my first two years of legal work are cemented in my memory. It was a side of life that I'd only read in books or seen in movies. Drug cartels. Terrorists. Mobsters. Murder. Playing even a small role helping prosecutors gather evidence to prove complex cases made my adrenaline race.

My bosses made the world a safer place. They fought for justice for those who couldn't fight for themselves.

I was hooked.

TAKING FLIGHT

Working hard isn't a chore when the magic ingredients are there.

- You love what you do
- Your work matters
- You like the people
- You feel valued and valuable
- You have champions and allies
- You continue to grow and aim high

Lucky for me, my early career had every magic ingredient in spades.

Yes, it was hard. The hours were long. Not every day was a dream. In fact, some sucked. I didn't make much money. School loans loomed large. Despite all that, I achieved something more important.

A purpose.

I felt worthy, empowered, and valued when my work helped other people, especially when they didn't have a voice or the ability to advocate for themselves.

After law school, I accepted a year clerkship with the Honorable Colleen Kollar-Kotelly, now a federal district court judge. At the time I clerked, she presided over complex cases in the local trial courts.

My judge, as I refer to her fondly, was smart, elegant, savvy, and kind. Her work ethic was beyond anything I had ever seen, even rivaling my mother. As a trailblazer who achieved many firsts, hard work was never optional. Breaking barriers was one thing, sustaining those achievements was another—especially with everyone watching. She was a stickler for being prepared and paying attention to the most minute details. They mattered to her, so it had better matter to you.

She wore stylish suits and beautiful jewelry. I did not. At first, she grudgingly tolerated my off-the-rack, untailored, frumpy, loose-fitting suits. It didn't last. When she invited me to go shopping, I was fully aware it wasn't really an "invitation." She had a hook. It was getting close to interview season. Game time again.

You can't show up looking like you are drowning in that suit, she argued. *If you want to be taken seriously as a woman,* she explained, *you not only need to be the best in the room, you need to look the part. Down to the shoes.*

A warrior suit with style.

THE PURPLE SUIT AND THE BIG DREAM

Watching serious criminal trials unfold in my judge's court-room cemented my dream to be a prosecutor. In Washington, DC, that meant the US Attorney's Office. The Office usually didn't hire right out of clerkships, but that year they made exceptions for three slots.

Much like my mom, Judge Kotelly would support your goals. She was keen to advise on strategy for your job search. But you were accountable for landing the opportunity and for owning your success.

After I applied for a prosecutor slot, I eagerly waited to see if I made it to the interview phase. Judge Kotelly thought it was important for me to meet then-US Attorney Eric H. Holder, Jr.

If your application is pending, he might as well know who you are, she pointed out. As luck would have it, as a former judge himself in the local courts, he was speaking at an upcoming judicial conference. It was the perfect place for a "low-key" introduction.

On the designated day, I showed up close to lunch hour wearing my newly tailored purple suit. Looking around, it seemed all the other judges had the same brilliant idea. The place was teaming with law clerks looking edgy.

Yet, there was an unexpected glitch. The morning conference panels ran late. US attorney Holder, the guy everyone was angling to meet, stayed on the stage chatting with former colleagues. He wasn't mingling. You could see confusion and restlessness wash over the crowd as Plan Bs were hatched.

Well, this won't do, my judge said. *We'll have to improvise. You need to crawl up on the stage.*

Horrified at the visual, I resisted.

If you know my judge, you know there are times when objections are pointless. This was one of those times. With a stern look, she leaned in and whispered, *This is no time to be a wallflower, my dear. Get up on that stage.* It wasn't a request.

There I was hiking up my fitted skirt, butt to the audience, crawling on stage in heels to meet the US attorney and future Attorney General of the United States. His look conveyed both surprise and amusement, no doubt aware of what I'd been up against as my judge looked on below. Introducing myself briefly, I gave my pitch. Several rounds of interviews later, I got the job.

At the age of twenty-six, this wide-eyed girl in the purple suit became a prosecutor.

It turns out with hard work, grit, resourcefulness, determination, attention to detail, courage, and some nudges from those rooting for you . . .

Dreams can come true if you
believe in yourself, overcome your fear,
and go for it.

CHAPTER 3

The Girl Becomes a Warrior

Amy Conway, on behalf of the United States . . .

The first time I said those words in court, it was surreal. Gripping the podium to keep my hands from shaking, I focused on keeping my voice strong. People were watching. Nerves had to stay hidden beneath my suit.

Every so often, I pinched myself to be sure I was awake.

THE NEWBIE

As a newbie, I had much to prove. I was energized by the constant motion of the courthouse. It was easy to embrace the challenges of plowing through piles of case files each day. The early months were a constant flow of low-level crimes like shoplifting, prostitution, assault, and drug possession. With experience, I graduated to guns and drug sales before more serious felonies and violent crimes.

The courthouse was like my second home. The building felt comfortable, the judges familiar. But, unlike my clerkship, I now had a lead role in the play unfolding in courtrooms each day. Sometimes cases went smoothly. Other days, they fell apart. There was no typical workday or work week. Expecting the unexpected came with the territory.

Over the next six years, I saw the best and the worst of humanity, acts of heroism, tragedy, and unmatched resilience. The job was equal parts exciting, grueling, frustrating, and rewarding.

You might wonder if *Law & Order* is close to reality? The answer is yes. The show does a pretty good job of capturing real-life drama. The difference, of course, is in real-life you must live it. Cases aren't over in an hour. The tears, anger, fear, pain, and frustration people experience are real. Lives are often at stake.

I felt responsible for making sure justice was served.

Inevitably, some days were harder to let go or erase from my memory. Even when I won.

THE YOUNG GIRL I NEVER FORGOT

For years, I specialized in crimes against women and children, from assault to rape and murder. One day, I had to cover the case of a four-year-old child. She died after a fall down the stairs. At least that's what her mother's boyfriend said. The problem was her small body was covered in bruises. His story didn't fit.

Cases like this are tough to prove, especially if no reliable eyewitnesses are available to say what happened. The mother wasn't talking. The other kids were too young. Certain the mother's boyfriend was the culprit, the police arrested him.

We had four hours until the court hearing. A judge would decide if the evidence was enough to keep the boyfriend in jail. We were laser focused.

As detectives were huddled in my office, the phone rang. The Medical Examiner's office had agreed to expedite the young girl's autopsy to find more clues. A technician told us to come over. They had something to show us.

I had never been to an autopsy before. To say I was nervous about the first one being a four-year-old child is an understatement. I honestly didn't know if I could handle it. At the same time, there was no way I could decline. Not only was it needed for court, I felt like it would dishonor her if the prosecutor handling her case wasn't as prepared as possible.

The Medical Examiner's office was an experience like no other. Eerily calm, the smell of death and chemicals is unmistakable. Walking in, the others seemed comfortable in a way that was unnerving. It was their business. I was glad my stomach was empty.

Standing in the cold room where the bodies lay, that strange putrid smell ever present, I had one of those chats with myself to keep calm and stay focused. The warrior in me compartmentalized my emotions to give my sleuthing brain room to do its job. We needed evidence for court. The clock was ticking.

As he worked, the medical examiner showed us the bruises that were not consistent with the boyfriend's story. Not all of them were fresh. This child had been abused over time. Next, he showed us the real discovery. The young girl's back was broken. A clean break from a blunt impact.

As one detective asked if it could be from the fall, his partner picked up on the clue. A strange pattern along her spine. It never had time to develop into a full-blown bruise. Inspecting it closely, his partner moved his fist along the area. There it was: the pattern consistent with the knuckles of a large man's fist.

The young girl had been punched so hard that her spine broke in two, a blow that sent her down the flight of stairs to her death. The cause of death was homicide.

A short time later, we were back in court. With photos and other evidence, we had enough to keep the boyfriend in jail. As the judge finished ruling, the bustle of the courtroom resumed. The boyfriend was led out in handcuffs. The defense attorney asked about a plea. The clerk called the next murder case.

After packing my bags and turning to leave, I stopped when I saw her.

The girl's mother was crying for the boyfriend.

Later that night, I cried for the young girl who lived and died alone.

These were the kinds of cases that got me up in the morning and kept me working late at night. It was exhausting work, but I didn't mind.

> Whenever I was tired, it was easy to remind myself of people who relied on me to get it right and the responsibility I had to speak for those unable to speak for themselves.

FIERCE ADVOCATES, THICK SKINS

Not all cases were solved that quickly. Some were more complicated, especially when witnesses were threatened not to testify, or a child was afraid to speak up, or a rape victim was too traumatized to re-live what happened. You had to be patient and meticulous, resourceful and persistent, strategic and tactical, fierce and compassionate.

Some witnesses were truthful. Others lied. Some had trouble remembering details. Seasoned detectives would say: *To build a strong case, you have to test everything you are told, even if it comes from the police.* As a prosecutor, it was your job to look at the minute details. You had to ask what the evidence proved, identify gaps, and call out what didn't make sense. No case was perfect. Ever.

In this world of fighting crime, men far outnumbered women. Still, there were many accomplished women. None of them were wall flowers. You couldn't afford to be.

Not surprisingly, boys' clubs and chauvinism most certainly existed. Ill-humored jokes and inappropriate stories were common. The number of times I was called "babe" or "sweetheart" roughly equaled the times I was called "ma'am." Being called a "tough bitch prosecutor" on the street was a compliment. Being called worse was a given. Foul language was frequently woven into colorful stories or reactions to crazy situations on the streets by civilians and police alike. At times, you found yourself using those same words yourself.

"Sensitivity training," as you might think of it in the corporate world, wasn't particularly high on anyone's list when you were talking with the drug dealer who was your key witness in a murder case, or the mother whose son was killed. In court, you tried to manage some of the more vulgar realities of life out of respect. Otherwise, you rolled with it. It was more important to do your job well.

As you can imagine, I developed a thick skin.

And, yes, for better or worse, I can curse with the best of them.

"THE MOMENT"

You'll know when it's time to leave. It will be unmistakable. This was advice a seasoned homicide prosecutor gave me as he packed boxes in his office.

His moment was on a Saturday during weekend court duty. It was a typical morning processing arrests from the night before. He described the windowless hallway leading to the lower-level courtroom that smelled like stale sweat, booze, and cigarettes. The hall lights flickered. The floors were wet from the snow tracked in from the street.

Just then, he noticed a woman stumbling out of the court-room. Still drunk or high from the night before, she whimpered, vomited, then staggered on. Eerily, no one stopped. The light continued to flicker. People stepped around her and the trail she left as if it was nothing. Just another casualty of life on the streets.

You'll know, he said shaking his head in disbelief at the memory. He was right.

My moment came on a busy day. My third back-to-back murder trial. This time it was a gang member who had settled a score, a senseless payback in a never-ending cycle of violence. As we broke trial for lunch, a detective's message disrupted my train of thought.

Back at the office, there was a new case—a college student murdered. After a botched initial investigation, specially trained detectives took over. With intense media attention, they had to move quickly. As I walked in, on my desk were the carefully laid out crime scene photos, the autopsy report, and the witness statements.

My brain clicked, making the transition from trial lawyer to sleuthing mode. We searched for clues, threads to pull, breadcrumbs to follow. We poked holes in theories, debated motives.

As the clock ticked, for some reason, the picture of the dead boy caught my eye. The cold hard look of death. His battered and broken body. The son of a grieving mom.

Just then, the sound of my beeper signaled the trial was ready to resume. I signed subpoenas, finished my sandwich, turned on trial mode, and left for court.

Later that night, I cried—for the boy, his mom, and me.

BITTERSWEET

I never understood how people could leave this job, until I did.

Still passionate about solving mysteries and pursuing justice, I noticed the revolving door of violent cases became both easier and harder. Over time, I learned to compartmentalize information and emotions. "Mission mode," I called it. A necessary evil to survive.

Compassion was critical, yet it couldn't overshadow the job of making sure those responsible were held to account in a court of law: A woman raped, her throat slit and shot once in the head as her toddler slept nearby. A woman attacked by a serial rapist in the bathroom of a popular bar. A child sexually assaulted by her mom's boyfriend who threatened her never to tell. A three-month-old baby whose hand was submerged in boiling water, her skin and flesh melted from her small hand. Her sin? Crying.

These were typical days, weeks, months, years.

At some point, it bothered me that I no longer cringed looking through bloody photographs or autopsy reports. I wasn't shocked at the depths people went to hurt each other. Yet, every now and then, I was reminded of their unlimited potential to surprise me.

So, as my brain clicked from the college boy to lunch and back to court that day, what struck me most was my ability to eat.

During my "moment" and the tears that followed, I decided, no matter how much I loved the job, I never wanted to become so hardened by the worst of humanity that I lost my ability to be horrified. Practical and realistic was one thing. Cynical and hardened was something else.

My last night as a prosecutor, after finishing my final memo, I turned in my badge to the midnight security officer. Walking outside, the air felt crisp. The streets were quiet.

Pausing briefly, I looked down the block toward the police station and courthouse, my second home.

Leaving was bittersweet. I loved that job. I always will.

I inhaled a deep breath of fresh air as I turned and walked away. It was time.

THE DARK SIDE

When prosecutors leave government service for private practice, the running joke is they've gone to the "dark side." No longer among the so-called "white hats" or justice seekers, the question is whether they can make the philosophical and practical transition to justice defender, a warrior of a different kind.

My transition had a learning curve, but it was manageable. Yes, I missed the job and mission. It was hard to lose the power of the subpoena and law enforcement as a partner, but you couldn't stay distracted for long.

The defense side forces you to be creative and challenged in new ways. Financial crimes like fraud, bribery, and money laundering have their own intrigue. They are mysteries of a different flavor. You learn quickly that power can corrupt no matter who you are or where life takes you. People are people.

In my new world, bullets sometimes came in the form of paper.

BOUNDARIES: THE LESSON OF THE BOX

One thing I never got used to was Big Law's obsession with pedigree and pecking order.

> I cared more about work ethic and the ability to deliver results than your law school, rank, or country club. The hungrier, the better.

When I started in Big Law, I was all-in to learn this new game, but it's safe to say I wasn't up for the pedigree, pecking order dance. I wasn't your typical lawyer seven years out of law school.

My bosses, Bill and Mark, whom I adore, loved to push the envelope. As they taught me the ways of Big Law, they loved to have some fun with the "new kid." I loved pushing back.

One morning, we were meeting prominent Washington lawyers about a case. Following my judge's advice, I dressed the part. A new coat. A chic fitted suit. Fashionable heels. I carried a small file of key documents in my briefcase. As I walked up to meet them in the lobby, you can imagine my surprise when they handed me "the box" full of documents. As the newbie, they said grinning, I had to carry it.

Holy crap, this thing is heavy, I thought as I struggled to get the box out of the cab. Already ten steps behind as the guys walked ahead, I wondered whether they'd filled it with weights. There was no way we needed all this stuff.

By the time I walked toward the outer building doors, I was already plotting my revenge. Men in fine suits shuffled in and out of the law firm's stately lobby. Ahead, Bill and Mark were almost inside.

A cardinal sin. It was perfect.

I waited briefly outside until they turned to see where I was. They looked momentarily puzzled. That's when, eye-to-eye through the glass and in the loudest possible voice, I stomped my heel on the cement and shouted in frustration: *Doesn't anyone hold the door open for a woman anymore?*

Never have I seen a bunch of men in fine suits move faster. The sea of bodies parted. Apologies were whispered. Doors opened.

As I walked inside, I handed the box to Mark and my brief-case to Bill. *That'll be the last time we do that,* I said proudly. *You guys need some manners.*

Well played, they laughed.

I never carried a box for them again. At least not because they dumped it on me.

It wasn't about the box, of course. Or even the door.

The "lesson of the box" was my good-natured way of throwing the flag. I may have been new to the firm, junior to them, not from an Ivy League school, and a girl, but I was an experienced, accomplished trial lawyer. I could go toe-to-toe with the best of them. If they wanted a low-level flunky to carry their bags, it wasn't going to be me. The pecking order stuff was silly.

And if I (or anyone else) was carrying a heavy box, which I am fully capable of doing when needed, they were sure as shit going to have some good manners and open the door. It's how my mother raised me. It's how I'm raising my son and my daughter.

Bill and Mark loved giving me grief. They were great sports about getting it back.

Yes, I had more to learn about the defense side and new ways of looking at cases. They were masters at their craft. But my experience, resourcefulness, investigative skills, and brain power made them better—and they knew it.

A DIFFERENT KIND OF STING OPERATION

I don't think I need to go take this trip, I told the Central Asian lawyer on the phone. He agreed the Russian-speaking men were unlikely to share incriminating information with a Western woman. Plus, it was the start of locust season when millions of bugs take to the skies, a natural phenomenon that seemed worth skipping.

We were investigating bribes. A senior executive was pushing the CEO to stop wasting money on us. After all, he had been a loyal soldier for years. There was nothing to see. The CEO imposed a five-day deadline. Totally unreasonable. The pressure was on.

Tell-tale signs of trouble in financial records and email told us we were close, yet clues stopped at a strange email address employees in Central Asia were using. It didn't belong to the company. In our minds, the question wasn't if bribes were being paid, it was how. And, of course, who was directing it.

I like plans that are simple yet thoughtful, tactical, and goal-oriented. I also like outsmarting people who think they are untouchable. Here's what we put in motion. Our local lawyer would interview the employees. Countryman to countryman. Simultaneously, another lawyer interviewed the supervisor in the Middle East to keep him busy. Computer experts stood by in Europe. Other team members in the U.S. passed on details to help the lawyers challenge ridiculous answers.

By 3:00 a.m. Washington, DC time, one employee caved. We couldn't give him time to think or call his boss. The computer guys worked their magic, imaging data once thought to be untouchable.

What was buried inside the account? A treasure trove of email messages and texts in various languages that detailed the scheme, transfers of money, secret accounts, and government officials.

The so-called loyal soldier had directed the bribes. Worse, he'd bragged to underlings that he talked the "stupid" CEO into tanking the investigation. That part was in English.

Let's just say nothing angers a CEO more than a buddy stabbing him in the back and then calling him stupid, a sad and twisted end to a relationship that never was.

It's truly amazing the dumb things people write when they think no one can see. I constantly have to remind them: *Yes, we read your emails. And we're pretty good at figuring out what's hidden.*

Discoveries like these made the drudgery of investigating paper cases more interesting. At times, when the clock was ticking, it could feel like a competitive sport. A race against time to expose bad apples before companies and executives became front page news.

LIFE IN THE BUBBLE

I look back on my early Big Law years as life in a bubble. The hours were crazy, but I had it pretty good.

My boss, Bill, was in the club of elite Department of Justice alumni who had their fingers in just about every juicy scandal that hit the newspapers—or through exceptional lawyering stayed below the radar. It was a time when the work flowed. None of it was boring.

The environment was different in the pace, the type of work, and the feel. Fast versus slower. Hardcore versus refined. Low budget versus upper crust. Diverse versus homogeneous. Mission versus big money. The cultures were vastly different.

And gender? Many of my bosses early in my career were women. Big Law was a sea of white men.

In the early Big Law years, my gender did not feel like a barrier. It seemed my work ethic and work quality spoke for itself. I had a ton of experience. They knew my value. I was treated well. Traveling the world, I had key roles on interesting, complex cases. I was taken under wings, sponsored and championed, invited to fine dinners with spouses and clients.

Only in hindsight, I realize now that I was protected, even sheltered, from the more frustrating Big Law business politics. Moreover, if gender barriers were there, I didn't see them. Whether that was by choice, necessity, or convenience, I was focused on fine-tuning my craft.

I didn't want to work for the big dogs. I wanted to compete with them.

While it was irritating seeing some of my male peers move further ahead faster at other firms, it was easy to rationalize. They were older. Many had been in the law firm game longer. Confident I'd get there, I didn't sweat it. With my prosecutor training, thick skin, and ability to navigate tough situations, I figured it was just a matter of time.

Little did I know bigger challenges, wake up calls, and reality checks lay ahead.

Gender would play a much greater role in my future than I'd ever imagined, especially as I achieved successes and climbed higher.

CHAPTER 4

The Warrior and The Greasy Pole

It was May 1, 2007, a beautiful spring day. At thirty-six weeks and in my third trimester, I was about to become a first-time mom at thirty-nine years old.

Over the last few weeks, I'd been wrapping things up. Projects, memos, and client requests. As a law firm partner, you couldn't just disappear. I had a few deliverables to finish before my alleged due date toward the end of May.

Feeling crummy, I realized the late night and overseas conference calls were taking their toll. My ankles were swollen, and my back hurt. Relieved to have the morning off, I looked forward to a nap after my regularly scheduled doctor appointment.

I'd like for you to go to Labor and Delivery for monitoring and rest, my doctor said.

Suspicious, I asked, *Can I rest at home?*

Walk or wheelchair? she said to shut down any resistance.

Don't worry. It doesn't mean the baby will come today, the nurse whispered softly.

Now waddling toward that side of the building, I went through my mental checklist of work I had to finish and made a few phone calls.

It's just for monitoring, I told my friend, Cynthia, a mom of four.

Oh really? she joked. *They just didn't want to argue with you. Guess who's having a baby today?*

Irritated, I mumbled, *I am not having a baby today. I'm not ready!* In fairness to me, it wasn't on the schedule. I can still hear Cynthia laughing.

As I arrived, a nurse handed me a gown and led me to what looked eerily like a delivery room. It's safe to say that's when full-blown panic set in.

The next two hours were a whirl of activity. I churned out a board presentation and a client memo, and returned emails, barking at anyone who interrupted my train of thought. Knowing it was better for me to focus on something other than labor, which terrified me, my husband smartly stayed out of the way. He still jokes that when the staff confiscated my computer, he saw claw marks where my fingers had been.

Guess what? I had a baby that day. Her name is Olivia Kathleen, in honor of two women warriors. Her fire-pistol great-grandmother and my mom.

PS: I also finished two projects and handed off the rest of my work in record time.

REALITIES OF PARTNER LIFE

A few years before I became a mom and shortly before I got married, I became a Big Law partner. But being a low-level service partner was not my idea of success. I was keenly aware that getting "a seat at that table" didn't mean much.

By the mid-2000s, many Big Law firms adopted a two-tier partnership system. Income partners were in the lower tier. Equity partners were in the upper tier where the real money and power lives.

This system allowed revenue-generating partners to make more money by multiples. By contrast, the lower tier was more of a training ground for those on the way up, and a holding point for those on their way down or not deemed worthy of equity status. A wide range of salaries exists within each tier, depending on your perceived value, like the rungs of a ladder.

When I first made partner, I was at the bottom of the income partner rung (also known as "service" partners). It's a step in the right direction, but it wasn't anything I aspired to be for long. Life wasn't any easier. You worked more hours and gained business development, administrative, and firm responsibilities. You were always at someone's beck and call, and you made less money. (Think taxes, buying into the business, and smaller bonuses.)

Among my Washington, DC litigation partners, I had no peers in the room in age or gender. I had no real power or voice. The first and only woman partner in over seven years, I was twenty years (or more) younger than most partners and decision-makers, and about ten years younger than a few closer to my age.

In those early years, the market was tightening, and leadership decisions put pressure on my partners. It's safe to say they weren't used to it and didn't like being closely managed by leadership or accountable in new ways. Tensions were visible. Long-time partners seemed on edge, unhappy, and vulnerable to decisions by Big Law management. Cultures were becoming more cutthroat. Bill was getting ready to retire.

Some of the guys looked out for me, which I was grateful for. But, make no mistake, my presence changed the dynamic of partner meetings and lunches. While I was fully comfortable in tough environments and bucking the system, it was awkward.

For the first time, I felt different. A girl had officially entered the boys' club. For some, it took a little getting used to, even if they liked me.

Mark did his best to help. But it's safe to say, at some point, we both felt the impact of Bill's transition, the shifting business priorities of Big Law, and the impact on the culture of our group.

By the time I became a mom and was three years into partnership, I was gunning for the upper tier.

THE WARRIOR MEETS THE GREASY POLE

When Olivia was about six weeks old, I was enjoying a peaceful afternoon while she napped. Her early health issues had resolved. Family visits were over. Emails and pictures done. The sound of her soft breathing was a gift from heaven.

When my cell phone rang unexpectedly, I grabbed the phone trying not to wake her. A very successful, senior male partner in leadership said he was calling to share the good news. I'd made it to Big Law equity partner, something he didn't think had been achieved by a woman on maternity leave. He congratulated me and welcomed me to "the club."

Before hanging up, he laughed and said something I've never forgotten:

Welcome to the top of one greasy pole and the bottom of another. You still have a way to go. Hold on tight!

Then, he was gone—literally and figuratively.

Staring at the phone, I thought, *Thank you, but WTF? A greasy pole!*

All those brutal years of working crazy hours, having no limits or balance, and I was at *the bottom of a greasy pole*? I hated the visual and found myself wishing for a ladder. It would have been easier on a gal wearing heels.

Worse, the partner's message made clear that I wasn't part of the "real" club. The uncertain climb would continue. It would also be slippery, dirty, and hard. One could never ease up or let go if you hoped to make it to the "top" (whatever that now meant).

Over the years, I hung on for the carrot of equity partner because I knew I had earned it. When I got over that hurdle, it was an honor and a relief.

Yet, now, being at the bottom of another "greasy pole" made me start to wonder if it was a real "win."

I later learned it wasn't.

A PAY GAP THE SIZE OF THE GRAND CANYON

On a pretty spring night, about a year or so after Jack was born, I sat outside a swanky bar having cocktails with mostly male alumni from the US Attorney's Office. They were all former prosecutors like me who had gone to the "dark side."

Given travel schedules, it's not always easy to meet up in person.

People were in a good mood. There was a lot of banter, laughter, tales of the old days. Even some new stories of the dumb stuff people say and do that get them into trouble. After a few drinks, the guys started talking business referrals and salaries. Listening, I was *stunned*.

I knew their referral network was better than mine. I also knew there was a pay gap. What I didn't expect was that the pay gap was the size of the Grand Canyon. In fact, they were so far ahead financially, it was embarrassing.

Not only had they negotiated substantially better salaries to start, but I continued to be paid way under market. My salary then was roughly half (or less) what they were making even though, in some years, I led bigger cases.

After a period of nursing my wounded ego, I invested time creating my business case, tracking billable hours, teams led, and revenue. I shared it with several more senior partners and mentors to make sure I wasn't missing anything. I wasn't.

I put on my warrior suit, clicked my brain to "mission mode," and scheduled a time to meet with a top leader of the firm.

The morning of our lunch meeting, I was incredibly nervous but ready. I'd paid attention to every detail. True to my training and Judge Kotelly's advice, I dressed the part, ready to make my case on my value.

This leader was a busy guy. I assumed he had no clue that I was so grossly underpaid. I figured when he saw the numbers, he'd be as surprised as I was. I wondered if the lunch he suggested at the Four Seasons was a good sign. The formal furniture in the lobby, tall ornate ceilings, and the color gold conveyed class, respect, money, power.

As I arrived, I saw he was already seated at a small round table in the middle of the room. He casually typed an email as the waiter hovered nearby. *A regular,* I remember thinking. *They seem to know him well, an important man who conducts business here often.*

After saying hello, we had the obligatory idle chitchat. He asked about my family, the kids, my colleagues. My stomach was in knots, yet the conversation seemed to put me at ease. We ordered. I kept it simple, light, easy. A salad. Iced tea.

Lunch arrived. That's when the whole mess started. He asked what I wanted to talk about.

My palms were sweating. My high heel clicked lightly against the floor under the fancy white tablecloth. I held my empty fork to keep my hand from shaking. The restaurant noise faded away. Silence. As if everyone was watching.

I began with the introduction I had practiced. He liked people who were direct but not whiny.

I wanted to talk with you about my practice, revenue, and compensation. I know it's getting to that time where you do annual reviews. There are some interesting things I thought you might want to know so I brought some data with me . . .

Before I finished the next few sentences on compensation, he took me by surprise. He wasn't shocked at all.

You're right, he said simply. His face relaxed.

Then, he explained this was how the system worked. My hard work and contributions were highly valued. They would pay off over my career. For now, though, the revenue I was generating helped pay for the greater good of the team, the salaries of those senior to me, and then those high-profile investments the firm was making to build more depth and strength.

He suggested that *I be patient.* I would see the rewards swing in the other direction by the time I was fifty.

He. Actually. Said that.

Trying to play it cool and keep my jaw from hitting the classic white salad plate, I remember thinking to myself, *Holy shit, at this pace, I could be dead by fifty.*

By that point, I realized how incredibly stupid I had been. Not only did I not have a seat at the real table, I was paying for the chair some guy was sitting in, along with his car and his kid's private school tuition.

I faced an uncomfortable realization sitting in that upscale restaurant with the man in the fine wool suit and red silk tie.

Partnership was business. Business was business. Big Law leadership and Big Law culture wouldn't always look out for those who were loyal, hard-working, resourceful, and reliable. Firms in the industry were taking risks and making bets. Firm leadership decided I had my place.

They were more than happy to take what I delivered, but they weren't yet willing to pay for it.

Soon after, I met my friend and executive recruiter, Jane Roberts. Jane is not only sought-after and highly regarded in the Washington, DC legal community, she is also an accomplished lawyer, extraordinarily busy mom, and the wife of Chief Justice John Roberts. I shared my story and showed Jane my numbers. She saw the whopping gaps immediately.

Jane reinforced one of my mom's most important lessons: to be accountable to myself.

In meeting after meeting, other Big Law leaders confirmed that I was substantially under-market. With the gift of Jane's sage advice and advocacy, I changed jobs and more than doubled my salary in a single year. For my own business strategy reasons, I didn't even take the highest offer.

I couldn't fix the past. But I could set a different course for the future—even if equality and a seat at the table of true power was still elusive.

TOUGH LESSONS ON BUSINESS

Another huge challenge for all lawyers is building business. In private law firms, your "book of business" and "client relationships" translate to money. To be successful, you must hustle.

For a woman, hustling is not a problem. We're used to that. But you had to get past two major hurdles.

- **Getting the work:** With few exceptions, most C-suite clients looked like my older partners. At the board level, they were almost exclusively men. That changed a little over the years, but the decision-makers I came across were rarely women. When it came time to dig them out of a hole, many leaders inherently defaulted to someone who looked familiar. While my track record allowed me to overcome some of that bias, like many women, gender and age remained an ever-present challenge.

- **Getting the credit:** Getting the work was only half the battle. As you compete for higher salaries, Big Law compensation is tied to credit. The partner's name in the revenue column is not always the person who leads the team or does the actual work. In this tougher game, you learn quickly: if you want to be paid, you must be willing to have difficult money conversations with your partners, especially for big money cases.

Here's how that can play out.

I led a case that started out small but wound up being more than $10 million. When the client asked our firm for advice, my partner discretely put my work under his client number to *limit the administrative paperwork*. The client number and the revenue associated with it are key to Big Law compensation. Think of it like this: Whoever keeps the "credit" in their revenue column receives the most compensation from those revenue dollars. For a $10 million case, that is a lot of money and hardly an "administrative" matter.

Within months, we were ramping up a big investigation with a growing team. The partner wanted to keep the credit even though he had nothing to do with it and never worked on it. It was *his relationship*, he said.

Big Law leadership, in their infinite wisdom, didn't want to upset the partner but promised it would work out. *Focus on the work*, they suggested. Guess who walked away with the credit *and* the cash for owning the work at compensation time? It wasn't me.

Over the years, I got better about advocating for myself. Some Big Law partners were truly fair and equitable. Yet, in years where people were worried about their own compensation or pipeline of work—or worse, had delicate egos—these tough conversations didn't always work out.

Was this problem exclusive for women? No. But it was harder for them for three reasons.

First, Big Law partnerships are notorious for showing a bias toward male partners to manage key business relationships, or for promoting male partners faster on compensation.

Second, women aren't always willing to stir the pot or bite the system that feeds them. We don't always negotiate well. Worse, mindful of being perceived as whiny, difficult, aggressive, or ambitious, we aren't as willing to go to the mat to call out inequality or unfairness.

Third, leadership doesn't always do the right thing when it comes to challenging a peer male partner. After all, they might need something from him down the line and memories can be long.

While I was fearless in defending my clients, I was always more hesitant when it came to advocating for myself in Big Law. Like most women, I wasn't among the inner circle, and self-advocacy from women wasn't always received well.

WORK HARDER ADVICE

Over time, as an "only" and, at times, "one of a few," I was eager for any advice, especially from highly accomplished women who came before me. This business was tough. Piling on motherhood was daunting. The gist of their advice was this:

Big Law is still male dominated with biases that hold women back.

Keep your head down and your foot on the gas.

Buy help at home wherever possible so you can focus on work.

Be available. Go the extra mile. Support any committees or business development efforts you can. (The fact that technology in my generation allowed us to work 24/7 without being physically in the office was an improvement.)

Never show you are struggling or go part-time. You'll get paid less, work just as hard, and find yourself on another track. You'll never make up the pay gap.

The advice was reality, they said. *A bitter pill we had to swallow.*

Do more with less time. Make it work. Don't complain. Sort of like a bad marriage.

I knew the reality was true. I had already made huge sacrifices and faced salary gaps. As I seemed to be finally nearing increased financial security, keeping my foot on the gas seemed like a no-brainer.

For better or worse, I forged ahead.

HARD REALITIES

The advice of working harder and being a team player and superwoman, while well-meaning, didn't equalize the playing field.

As I look back, the advice played into an already unequal system and allowed the bar to be set higher. By taking the advice, I was encouraged to set the bar even higher for myself, a vicious cycle that made the greasy pole climb even more slippery.

What no one really prepares you for is this:

When you are the cool, hardworking up-and-comer, the system and male power figures are more than happy to promote women. As women become competition, the game shifts. It gets infinitely more complicated. Grittier. Tougher. At times, dirtier.

That latter greasy pole game is all about power and money. The haves and the have nots. As you become more successful, the game is about something even bigger. If equality is real, it is about what the haves must share—or even give up—when money and power are legitimately earned by others.

While I knew I would never make up the total pay gap, I thought closing the gap would bring me closer to a more equitable game. That the climb would get easier.

In some ways, thankfully, it did. I began to gain financial security, a move that would prove critical later.

In other ways, the climb got harder, more endless, and a heck of a lot lonelier.

When I changed law firms, I was firmly alone in a new world with even fewer women at my level in the entire firm. Eyes were watching from all directions, wondering who I was and whether I would have the chops to deliver on the bet their leadership had made.

Some were okay. Some weren't happy. Some were skeptical. Some were jealous. Some waited to see what this new girl in a new sea of men could bring to their table.

The best visual I can conjure up is this:

> *The girl climbing the greasy pole finds a small platform. A welcome respite. The mission, dreams, expectations, pressures, and judgments hang heavy from her shoulders. Like uneven weights on the scales of justice. Then, summoning her courage, she straightens her skirt, and buttons her jacket. She inhales deeply, rebalancing her load. She flexes her hands. Alone, she begins to make the greasy pole climb again. Ever mindful of the hungry sharks in the waters below. And with eyes forever watching her. . . .*

PART II
THE GAME

*Just because you carry it well
doesn't mean it's not heavy.*

—VICTORIA GARRICK

*Friend: Are you getting enough sleep?
Me: Sometimes. When I sneeze my eyes close.*

—YOUR TANGO

CHAPTER 5

The Ruse

When you are the only woman or one of a few, you have to be excellent. Every minute. Every day. You can't turn it off. You can't make mistakes. That is why I never had kids.

These were the words of a senior woman executive at a diversity event in New York.

I was the "host," a last-minute command performance requested by some of my male partners who promoted the event as an opportunity to learn how women succeed in business and law.

The guests? Women executive clients of the firm. The audience? Associates, counsel, partners. Women and men.

Looking at the faces of the women near the front of the makeshift stage, I cringed. Some shifted uncomfortably in their chairs. Others whispered outside my line of sight. I could only imagine what was going through the minds of the young women, the moms, or those wanting to be moms. I wanted to hug them.

It got worse.

The executive explained that her husband didn't have a job and made sure her life ran smoothly. Essentially, he was her caretaker.

Sensing anxiety rising in the audience, the next woman executive over-corrected. She seemed to want to assure women that one could have a career and be a mom.

I am a mom, and I have a successful career. It's hard. But it can be done. I work extra hard to be excellent in both roles. If my daughter needs brownies for school and I have a big project, I will stay at work until 3:00 a.m., take a cab home, make the brownies by hand, and then go back to work. You can do it all!

A nervous young woman up front asked about a personal life. Both woman executives laughed. *No*, they said. *Not even close. There is no life really. There's no such thing as work-life balance.*

By now, I wanted to strangle my male partners in the back of the room. Their beaming smiles revealed how utterly clueless they were. It's clear they hadn't given any thought to the program messaging.

If they were looking to inspire anyone, myself included, they failed miserably.

I failed too.

As I sat there, microphone in hand, I couldn't reassure anyone that I had a personal life either. Far from it. My juggling act was in full swing. Worse, I wasn't completely honest about how hard it was, how I struggled, or how nutty my schedule had become.

I wasn't at quite the level of the brownie executive, but I wasn't that far off from her either. The only difference was I'd buy the brownies and selfishly take the two hours of sleep.

EXCELLENCE

While I didn't love the discussion that day about choices on motherhood, what the women executives said about "excellence" was true.

A woman did in fact have to be excellent—even beyond excellent—to have the privilege of getting to *the bottom* of the greasy pole. A woman had to excel even further to crawl up that damn thing.

It took muscle, blood, sweat, grit, resourcefulness. All while looking like a lady in nice heels and a suit. Under a spotlight with all eyes watching. Some hoped you would succeed. Others hoped you would slip.

Senior women explained to me over time that excellence meant something different for women than for their male peers in any job or industry. Mistakes or missteps matter for everyone, but they can be more costly when you are an "only" or "one of a few."

What might be viewed as a learning experience for male peers could prove tougher for a woman. It could be the proof others were looking for to show you didn't belong. Or weren't ready. Or weren't the right one to pick for the few chairs made available.

In this cutthroat world, you didn't want to become "that girl."

I'd seen more than one woman fall victim to harsh criticism when someone felt she hadn't measured up.

One legendary story involved a massive government investigation. A highly regarded woman defense attorney allegedly failed to deliver a key document to the government. It was corrected, but it created some bad blood with the government and among the team. Of course, the lead team was packed with senior firm leaders who were men.

If bad documents are known in big investigations, no decision to give or not give a potentially incriminating email is ever made alone. I knew the backstory. The woman was an easy scapegoat. The legend of "her mistake" lived on for years. In the story as retold, the men were blameless.

These challenges aren't limited to law.

The spotlight on women who break barriers is brutal. Making a mistake or getting blamed for errors can end a career quickly.

Yes, men must work hard. But the expectations, demands, pressures, and spotlight on women is harsher and less forgiving.

THE ART OF JUGGLING

Another truth in the women executives' comments was the importance of the art of juggling, a skill I learned to excel at as a prosecutor. After partnership and motherhood, I mastered it.

It was hard for anyone to truly appreciate what I could get done on any given day. Similar to many women, I didn't announce what I could do nor the invisible tasks at home or work. My husband didn't realize it until he took a hiatus from work. Even then, many of my invisible tasks continued. Over time, they were an expected part of my job.

Like the brownie executive at the diversity panel, I overcompensated. I didn't want my gender or motherhood to be seen as a limitation. Plus, there are things that simply default to moms, like planning, school emails, or sick kids.

What does the art of juggling look like? This is one of many doozies:

> It was a chilly winter morning in early 2014. After seven months of commuting to Europe almost every week from Monday to Friday, the team and I were preparing a big presentation. It was "all-hands-on-deck."

My husband, Sid, left for an early morning test flight. I was working from home when my six-year-old daughter, Olivia, woke up with a stomachache that quickly turned into a scene from *The Exorcist*.

Although my clothes were covered in God knows what, I still remember stepping between the shoes of "mom-of-sick kid" and "badass warrior lawyer" as the never-ending wave of conference calls continued uninterrupted. Poor Olivia curled up on towels in our bedroom, napping off and on.

Suddenly, out of nowhere, our au pair, followed by the painter, appeared in the doorway just as the pediatrician was calling. In a split second, my universe shifted.

The pediatrician told me to get Olivia to the hospital. The au pair, holding her jaw in pain, needed an emergency root canal. Our painter, covered in white plaster, gave me a "head's up" that our hallway ceiling had just caved in.

Texting my team and client, I dropped everything and put on my superhero mom cape. I remember calling in the cavalry, securing a school pickup for young Jack. Driving to the emergency room as Olivia held her bucket, I whispered over and over: *It's just another day. You can do it. Balls in the air. . . .*

Lucky for me, everything came together. After some fluids and medicine, Olivia started to feel better. The au pair got her root canal. The painter fixed the ceiling.

And that big presentation?

Several weeks later, after three long days presenting to five government agencies, they agreed not to pursue criminal charges. The civil resolution, once threatened as north of $100 million, was finalized south of $10 million.

Not every day was as bad as the exorcist day, although some certainly felt like it.

Like another time I gave a presentation to a board of directors by phone while cradling one-year-old Jack. A snowstorm grounded flights, forcing a conference call. Jack had double pneumonia and finally fell asleep in my arms as the call came through.

Afraid he'd cry if I put him down, I powered through my presentation. I laugh at the visual now. There I was covered in snot and drool cradling a sick kid. The older, all-male board never knew. Neither did my partners.

Days like that made "mini crises," like last-minute school projects or skinned knees, seem like a snap.

They were hard yet sadly became effortless at the same time.

HIGH-SPEED HIGHWAYS AND SUPERHERO FEATS BECOME THE NORM

By the second decade of Big Law practice, my brain no longer clicked from sleuthing mode to advocacy mode to strategic mode to mom mode.

As more was required at work and home, my brain evolved to a complex, wildly efficient command center that managed multiple lanes of highway. All at once. All at high speeds. All with navigation and risk management demands that never turned off.

As the system expanded, I didn't realize then how much I was betraying myself. A never-ending illusion of doing it all.

My life became a spreadsheet. I could do anything with project plans, calendars, nannies, mom friends, and layers of costumes under my warrior suit to fit just about any occasion. I believed I could change lanes on the highway with great ease.

- Getting called away to a meet with a "whistleblower" in South America to learn what certain company executives were up to, and then shifting to another lane late that night to arrange summer camps

- Or moving from the fast lane where executives grilled me on case strategies, to a winding section of highway involving a planned scavenger hunt to find a puppy Santa left in Georgia after our beloved dog died from cancer

- Or careening from the middle lane during a complex interview with a senior executive to the emergency lane for a call about my son's bus accident

In a weird way, I felt immense pride when I pulled off an impossible working mom feat. There was a time I even believed the myth that women can do it all, be it all, have it all.

I'd fist bump myself in the living room, getting my coffee, driving in the car. I'd do backflips in my head. But alas. Victories were short-lived.

There was always another case, another crisis, another family challenge. The high-speed traffic never seemed to end.

Pretending that it was nothing or eminently doable just got harder. But there was more. We had to pretend at work too.

DIVERSITY RUSE

Getting called to perform at or to attend events and activities like the diversity panel were routine for women partners like me.

A lot of industries struggle with diversity. Big Law is notoriously bad at retaining women, especially among the upper equity tiers. Very few women make it to the top of that greasy pole. I gritted my way to just about the middle. It helps to trot out women who made it that far to prove women are welcome. That they can in fact "succeed."

Diversity programs are intended to make business cultures more inclusive of different backgrounds and open opportunities to all professionals, especially those who have been traditionally overlooked.

While there is great fanfare about Big Law's commitment to the advancement of women, the world looks different behind the curtain.

I'm the co-lead of an important department, yet I'm doing administrative work, lamented a female friend in leadership, *like approving expenses, taking minutes of meetings, and writing agendas.*

Her "leadership" position was taking precious time from doing her work and building her own business opportunities.

Leaders said the position was good exposure and training. But anyone could do this administrative stuff, she said. While she handled mundane tasks, her male co-lead, who was paid multiples more, showed up for business and strategy decisions. At the leadership table, she had half a chair. Her voice? No more than a whisper.

How does the position help you then? I asked.

It doesn't, she said. *What no one says out loud is that leadership positions aren't always real. And they don't translate to business or money or real responsibility or the ability to make positive systemic changes for women. I'm just doing administrative junk work they don't want to do.*

Like my friend, I was asked to help lead a department one year. Sort of. The man leading the team liked the title but was a terrible leader. Management didn't have the heart to remove him.

> *We'd love it if you could run things "behind the scenes,"* they said. *The department could use your expertise and management. At some point, we'll have a conversation with him. For now, we'd like you to do this quietly. Make him look good.*

I agreed to work with him as a peer but not quietly for him. Not surprisingly, his ego wouldn't allow it. I declined the "behind the scenes" role to make him look good. Management was stuck with him.

Women leaders can and do play important roles in organizations at all levels. In fact, some Big Law firms have actual senior women leaders in place. Yet, like corporate America, those percentages are still dismal. Unfortunately, to understand the real story on diversity and the advancement of women, one must look behind what organization's report. Even then, one must make sure the numbers and the people tell the truth.

In my experience, women not only pretend our lives are doable to meet the high standards Big Law sets for us, we have to lie or shade the truth about the systems we live in. And we do.

We not only have to be quietly excellent and juggle a gazillion balls to climb a greasy pole in a tough, unequal system. We have to say it's not tough and unequal.

We tell other women, clients, and the world that the pole we climb isn't all that greasy nor are we climbing it alone. We have a team! Men in our orbit understand our struggles! Our organizations support us! We are treated equally!

This is the part of the gig I found most distasteful. Yet, I played along too.

It's time for some truth here. (Yes, we need to say it out loud. Not just in an anonymous survey.)

The truth is teams are often cutthroat and individuals self-interested. Success is measured in ways that disadvantage women and working moms. Our struggles are not understood because we have to say Big Law is doing a great job giving us opportunities. We have to say our male peers understand the challenges in our climbs when, in truth, they don't.

I could write an entire book about countless diversity scenarios based on my own experiences and women friends. Here's one example.

Another early morning travel day. *At least I'll be home by dinner,* I told myself.

My 6:00 a.m. flight from Washington, DC to Indiana landed at 7:30 a.m. Just enough time to grab coffee and read pitch materials before my partners landed from different cities. Six partners. Four men, two women. This opportunity was worth millions of dollars in business.

The materials display a nice mix of faces, I noticed. *I hope the client doesn't ask too many questions about our diversity track record, like how many women stay or leave, how many are actual equity partners or in leadership. . . .*

A short time later at the planning meeting in the airport lounge, the group decided the two women and top-paid guy would speak about the firm's diversity program strengths, something the client cared about.

I had done this before. An age-old speech. Yet, this time, I felt uneasy. My firm struggled with diversity. Everyone knew it. Of the precious few women in the equity ranks, none were near the top of the pay scale. Women also faced greater risk of slipping down the pole in tight years, like the year we were having.

Our forty-five-minute client meeting started on time. Around the table were a few men and senior women from our client. Time was short, so we got right to the agenda. After discussing our backgrounds, experience, and the company's legal needs, we answered some questions. Then, we moved to special pricing. Next, diversity.

When our top-paid guy started throwing out diversity statistics and the support for women, I almost fell over. They were total BS. *Did he not know the real numbers? Did he live on the same planet we did?* I wondered. Yet, without missing a beat, the rest of us jumped in heaping praise on each other, our firm, and our leadership.

Everyone at the table nodded, soaking in the stuff we were shoveling, proud to be in the room with each other. The client seemed to love it.

I wanted to throw up. We sounded like cheesy used-car salesmen selling an old Buick with no working heater and a cracked muffler held up by a thin wire.

After we patted each other's backs and parted to catch flights home, I called another woman partner from the airport to ask what she thought.

> *We must do whatever is needed to get in the room and get the business,* she said. *Our clients aren't dumb. They know the truth. If we get the men to say it, we all figure they have to start living equality someday.*

Later, I called another close friend and client. *What do you think? Did anyone buy the lies? Did clients lie about their programs too?*

> *It's getting better, but yes,* she said. *We see the statistics about women in law. We know the position you're in. Everyone lies in those meetings. Everyone knows the drill. It's sales. We shade the truth about our experiences too.*

The terrible statistics my friend mentioned were those tracked by legal publications, like Law360. In 2021, Law360 reported that in the last six years, the number of women equity partners only rose from 19.2 percent to 23.3 percent. A sad statistic when we know many of those women weren't at the high-end of the salary charts nor in power positions and remain underpaid—and that even some of those women are still choosing to leave.

My firm's average at the time of that pitch *didn't even reach* the low industry norms. Yet, year after year, we delivered speeches shoveling the same lies or selling the same stories in shades of a color that shouldn't even qualify as gray.

SURVIVAL AND ADAPTABILITY

To me, Big Law came to symbolize a rigid system, ever resistant to change that required women to be adaptable and flexible in infinite ways. Women who stayed learned to accommodate that system to accept what it was willing to offer. Even if unequal, the pay was good.

But there was a cost to buying into the game and the system. A team player couldn't say no to championing your organization's "successes" or how the system supported us.

On some warped level, playing our roles seemed to make everyone feel better.

The "have nots" could believe that someday these programs might actually grow some teeth and work.

The "haves" could hope what they were doing was "enough." After all, leaders today didn't create the system they now have to fix. It must be exhausting for them to carry the burden they inherited from the men who came before them (along with greater promotional opportunities, higher pay, client relationships, revenue, and business).

And therein lies part of the problem: Inheritance.

Another part of the problem is that Big Law leaders allow it to continue. Sadly, with some unwitting help from us women who accommodate them.

While I know some men who were truly, genuinely, and selflessly committed to equality—and they should be celebrated—they were not among the majority. More often, an interesting split existed.

Seeing the universal value in giving junior women bigger pathways to advance allowed us to easily rally around that cause, even though the commitment of resources was thin.

Equality at higher levels was infinitely more complicated. That's where women met greater resistance to evening the playing field. Why? Because, at that level, for equality to be real, it requires some redistribution of power and money.

This is also where women, myself included, abdicated or fell short on important advocacy. We'd invest in arguing for change for those below us. We had a much harder time speaking up for ourselves.

We'd admit the truth to each other privately. Encourage each other to soldier on. Focus on survival in the long game.

Over time, to fulfill all these roles, I became a chameleon warrior of sorts. Adapting to the person Big Law, my peers, and even clients needed me to be became a necessary survival tool in a world focused on money, power, and a structural hierarchy that looked nothing like me.

In my idealist world, I wanted to believe change was possible, that my continued participation could make things better.

As years went by though, it felt increasingly hypocritical championing a system with a greasy pole that didn't willingly and equally reward women for the hard work and excellence the system demanded.

I didn't speak up, not wanting to rock the boat or put what I had achieved at risk. None of us did, really.

In the years leading up to the pandemic, my warrior suit fraying, friends and clients with front row seats warned that my pace would catch up with me.

I didn't listen. I stubbornly clung to the fantasy that women could have it all. I was still trying to prove my worth to Big Law.

My reckoning would come.

CHAPTER 6

A World Gone Mad

You know the fall will be busy, right? my husband joked as we
hustled the kids out the door for dinner in Rome, Italy. *Every
time we take a great vacation, you wind up with a big case by
the time it's over. It's like clockwork.*

He wasn't wrong. But I wasn't going to let work ruin this
once-in-a-life-time trip.

That night, we were meeting up with a large crew of friends
for a family-style dinner. I'd been dreaming of pasta dripping
with homemade red sauce, fresh olive oil, parmesan cheese,
prosciutto, fresh tomatoes, and basil. Carafes of local Italian
red wine. Gelato by the bucket.

I wanted a restaurant that catered to locals. Something
tucked away, unpretentious, yet classy. My fiftieth birthday.
About eight years after that crazy Four Seasons lunch. It was
a milestone I wanted to remember.

As we wandered down steamy cobblestone streets with no
signs, we stumbled across an alleyway that vaguely matched

the map our hotel concierge drew for us. There, we saw the door. Non-descript. Low key. Almost hidden. It was perfect.

Peeking inside, we knew we were in the right place. The owner, an older gentleman with a booming voice said, *Buona sera, Signora. Buon compleanno!* He'd been expecting us.

Two large wooden tables awaited, arranged in an L shape so kids and adults could be together yet apart. Friends from the US and Europe trickled in, eighteen in total. Some of my favorite people. Our beloved au pair, Vivi, and her family from Germany. Close friends I cherished from home.

We talked, shared stories, laughed, grazed on antipasti, sipped incredible house red wine, and watched our kids exchange card tricks with the owner and his staff. The owner serenaded us in a deep, bellowing voice. As if by magic, large bowls arrived with piles of the freshest pasta, the two in the middle covered in a sweet-smelling, brilliant red sauce that matched visions from my dreams.

At home, we would have devoured this meal in earnest. Not tonight. No one was in a hurry.

Locals smiled as they found their favorite corners. Candles flickered. Conversation tones sounded like music. We didn't have a care in the world. In a restaurant across a vast ocean, we blended in among the locals at a small family restaurant buzzing with the sounds of music, friendship, family, love, warmth, and community. We lost track of time.

So, this is how real people live, I thought.

For someone who tracks her life in six-minute increments, this was heaven. I could have stayed forever, however long forever could last.

That was my life for almost three weeks. From Rome, we journeyed to a villa in Tuscany near a medieval town called Greve in Chianti, a town where more friends gathered to wander amidst lavender, gentle rolling hills, ancient towns, and to share dinners on old stone patios over endless nights under starlit skies.

And, yes, Sid was right. Not one, but three messy cases.

BEST LAID PLANS

In the months leading up to Italy, I fretted about work. The climb was brutal, yet my career seemed to be going strong. Then again, you never know in Big Law.

One year, the phones ring off the hook and you have no time to breathe. You are celebrated. Another year, exhausted, you live in fear, judgment, and scrutiny when phones ring less often. It's easy to drift from favored child to "sad disappointment" in no time. Those dreaded "down years" when the grease on the pole is slipperier.

After a strong start at my newest firm, I'd had a stretch where I was deep in the hunt for new cases. I was up against a compensation dip. Silent scrutiny and slippage stinks. It means another year of climbing back to where you were instead of moving up.

Sid had had enough. We were stretched too thin. Given my salary, he decided to step back from flying and regular work. In his career, he worked on some of the most sophisticated and exciting flight systems in the world. He loved his career. Yet, he thought the family would be better off if one of us stayed home.

After celebrating his "final" flight, he traded his wings for a carpool pass. The plan was for me to go all-in on my career.

By 2019, Italy and heaven was a distant memory.

BURNING THE CANDLE AT BOTH ENDS

In the first four months of 2019, I bounced between Europe, New York, Colorado, Minnesota, Tennessee, Virginia, the Northeast corridor, and Washington, DC. Asia beckoned in May.

- I led a team defending a company in a complex criminal investigation, developed and launched plans for a global anti-corruption compliance review across Europe and Asia, gave speeches in conferences and conducted panels on the advancement of women in law, and negotiated a settlement in an ethics investigation.

- I conducted interviews with witnesses and so-called whistleblowers, evaluated strategic options regarding employment laws in various countries, addressed daily client crises, studied complex data from arcane accounting and business operations systems, oversaw extensive document reviews, reviewed memos analyzing evidence collected across US states and faraway countries.

- I developed strategic plans to address legal challenges with government prosecutors and assessed political and strategic maneuvering among management teams and boards of directors.

- I confronted witnesses, navigated insecurities, listened with compassion to those who felt stomped on, ignored, or abused in their workplaces.

I answered calls and emails at all hours of the day and night.

My schedule was so ridiculous that my family refers to our March spring break ski trip as another "mom non-vacation."

I'd start work at 2:00 a.m., get Sid and the kids off to ski by 8:00 a.m., and work until 11:00 a.m. A brief nap. I'd meet the family for a couple of hours. We'd take a few hours to rest before fun family dinners. Then, I'd sneak in a couple more emails and start again. Of course, my phone was always with me, a must for the inevitable work calls or emails that rolled in.

By April, more than one client faced crises. One client had been under investigation for years without realizing it. The government was way ahead on time and low on patience. In these situations, the government always has the upper hand. If they say jump, you jump, buying time where you can yet knowing you'll never have enough time. It's a tough place for any client. At the same time, another client was involved in high-stakes settlement discussions. Another had management and operational changes, leadership turnovers, and challenges that seemed to be popping up all over the globe. Tensions were high everywhere.

Unfortunately, my clients weren't the only ones facing hard times. So was my family.

DOUBLE STANDARDS

When Sid set aside his career, neither of us anticipated how tough life would get. Within months of trading in his wings, he found he missed the mission, people, and purpose he'd been passionate about for decades.

The demands of home were a bigger grind than he imagined. The intensity of school moms, carpool, the schedules, and moods of preteen kids was all weirdly complex and even less predictable than the Presidential Helicopter Test program, he'd joke.

I had been warned about tough transitions by a retirement counsellor lady, the one I almost throttled after our meeting in the crocked house she called an office building. Part of the work "exit" process offered by Sid's company.

The lady was about fifteen years older than me. A different generation. As I sat in a stale-smelling, old stuffed chair on warped floorboards, I had a bad feeling about her. Only five minutes in, and my foot tapped in frustration.

When men leave work, she explained, *they need time to adjust. It will be your job to give him plenty of support.*

She went on to explain the *fragility of the male ego, how men need time and space to adjust in retirement, how women need to support them.* She suggested that *we not discuss money or home responsibilities for six months.*

You know my husband is leaving his job so that I can focus on my career? As in, he's taking care of the kids? I offered.

This makes it even more essential to give him room, make him feel important, give him support, line up some sitters. Make sure to give him time off, she offered.

Even though I wanted to shake her to wake her up, I'll concede her words made me nervous.

While Sid and I laughed about her double standards and whole-heartedly agreed her advice wasn't relevant to us, it was a foreshadowing of many double standards we didn't anticipate, and a window into challenges we'd face navigating new family dynamics and stereotypes that society ascribes to mothers and fathers, regardless of who is working in an office building.

Not only did I have to pretend at work, I had to pretend outside too.

My home load didn't get lighter. Despite our best intentions, it was worse.

Sid and I quickly learned that not everyone pays attention to a dad being in charge. Schools, teachers, doctors' offices, coaches, camps, and other moms more often default to "the mom." No matter what one does to redirect them.

When we were both working, neither of us noticed as much. When Sid was on point at home, it was unmistakable.

Jack having issues at school? The teacher calls the mom.

Arguing the case for Jack to move beyond his grade in certain subjects? Call in the mom.

Evaluating new schools that could meet Jack's academic needs? Where's the mom?

When Olivia fretted over a mysterious cyst on our young dog Bella's paw? Mom's phone rings. The pup's unexpected cancer diagnosis? Call in the mom.

Need cupcakes for school? Birthday party information? Snacks for volleyball? Forgotten field trip permission slips? *Mom! Mom! Mom!*

I remember seeing a cartoon one time where a mom was surrounded by a bunch of word bubbles, all with the word "Mom!" Disheveled, the mom's forehead was on the table. Rubbing her temples with one hand, she held up a white flag with the other. That was me.

Despite the intense travel and work schedule that would bring just about anyone to their knees, I had a full plate at home too. Sid worked hard to redirect, but there was only so much he could do while also managing his own feelings around the change in his "job."

In the past, I always rallied. We divided the work. It was hard for him to see that same distribution now crushed me.

While many of my male colleagues went home to relax or be with family on nights or weekends, I'd come home to "mom" jobs. Lists of problems to be solved, disagreements to be addressed, chores to be done, schedules to be managed, camps or schools to be found. Sid covered day-to-day juggling. Yet, there were many "invisible" and even some visible tasks that remained with me.

Before some of my trips, Jack would block me from leaving and scream, *I hate your job! You spend more time with those people than with me! You're always gone!*

No longer a heart-breaking toddler scene where your little one wraps their arms around your legs. Now a smart preteen kid, Jack was articulate and persistent.

Worse, he had a phone. It didn't always end at the door.

LIFE DELIVERS THE UNEXPECTED

If the work schedule and family challenges weren't enough, life delivered an unexpected bombshell.

Your dad is really sick. . . . My warrior mom's voice cracked over the phone through her tears.

Mom, I can't understand you. Can you slow down? Where are you? Did you call 911? I asked, trying to keep my voice calm as my heart pounded heavy in my chest.

Mom took in a few deep breaths, and then said, *He was catatonic when I found him, but I was able to get him down the stairs to the car. We're waiting at urgent care for an ambulance. He's out of it. Can you come home?*

I'm on my way. Text me where to go. I'll catch a flight. I love you, Mom. Hang in there. Hug Dad for me. Tell him I'm coming, I said with confidence as my hands shook.

It was one of the few weekends when I had a break in my grueling schedule. I called my siblings, packed my bags, hugged my family, cancelled my trip to Asia, and caught the next flight to Connecticut.

Over the next two weeks, my dad was gravely ill with encephalitis, an infection that ravages your brain. At first, we had no way of knowing whether he would live. But then, we faced the bitter pill that he'd never come home. The infection accelerated the progression of Alzheimer's, a nasty disease that eats away at your memory and regular brain functioning.

My once witty dad who was never at a loss for stories now struggled to find simple words. Some days were worse than others. In the span of weeks, my family since birth and the world we knew changed forever.

And another surprise.

> *Your dog has cancer,* the vet said in a matter-of-fact tone to me and Olivia. *She'll likely need surgery, but I'm not sure it will save her paw.*

> As Olivia began to well up with tears, I said, *Perhaps we could talk about this privately.* The last thing I needed was for him to talk about a life expectancy that might cause Olivia to lose it completely.

While we were navigating my dad's health crisis, Sid and the kids were nursing Bella back to health. The cyst that was cancer was removed in a tough surgery that almost destroyed the blood flow to her back leg. Following weeks of daily vet visits and wet wrap changes to heal the gaping surgical wound, Bella seemed to be regaining the use of her leg minus a toe.

Everyone was exhausted.

As my travels resumed, it felt odd but good to be back in a world I understood. Yet, now, I had a regular flow of family calls as I sat with witnesses or clients. Unhappy, on some days my dad called my phone ten, even twenty times. Leaving messages to let me know he'd felt abandoned. He remembered few of them.

ALL-HANDS-ON-DECK

By mid-summer, it was "all-hands-on-deck" at work. Again.

This time we were preparing for head-to-head sparring with the government to see how much maneuvering could be done to avoid the worst of all outcomes while trying to achieve the best of outcomes.

It is a time in a case when everyone works 24/7. Exhausting, yet invigorating in a weird way, it's when the pieces of the puzzle come together. A unique window of opportunity to think through creative solutions. You pull threads, think about "what ifs," and move the chess pieces around the board.

It's also a high-stakes, adrenaline-filled competition. The government has the upper hand, the ultimate trump cards. Yet, there are important ways we defense lawyers can score wins—from limiting onerous settlement requirements, to removing aggravating facts that can multiply penalties by the tens of millions, to reducing admissions that can spur civil litigation, lead to bad press, or destroy customer relationships.

This is when we lawyers must stay focused, keep everyone's eye on priorities, and prepare for contingencies if plans fall apart.

This was about when another bombshell dropped.

We don't like the look of your mammogram. We need you to come back for more tests, the doctor said staring at the imaging screen.

Okay. Is this the same routine I always go through? I asked checking my phone to see what emails I'd missed during my appointment.

I'm afraid not. We don't know one way or the other. We'll arrange the biopsy for next week, she said.

I put down my phone.

As I prepared for work battles, managed "normal" Big Law drama, and coped with family crises, I had a series of tests to rule out breast cancer.

The good news is we don't think it's cancer right now, my doctor said. *The bad news is that the tissue needs to come out. It's not an urgent emergency so you can take a few weeks, but I don't want you to put it off too long,* the surgeon said.

So, Christmas is out? I asked.

Yes, she laughed, *you can't wait that long. I'll expect you this fall.*

Is November still fall for you, I asked?

I saw her sigh, rolling her eyes, a slight smile. No doubt thinking to herself, another Washington lawyer.

It sounds so silly now, but I assure you putting off surgery made perfect sense at the time. Once I was assured surgery wasn't a "*serious* emergency," I didn't want to derail settlement discussions.

The real problem though was that I knew I couldn't handle a bad result if it came. Luck didn't seem to be going my way lately. Waiting gave me some time to process everything that had happened.

And so, days after we reached the key terms of a settlement agreement in early November, I was scheduled for surgery.

In a weird, ironic twist of fate, my friend and colleague on the case wound up in the same hospital suddenly and seriously ill. He would recover, but it was a rough time. We were in the same building on different floors.

He was on a morphine drip, and I was getting some loopy valium drip when I called him.

> *I'm looking forward to my date with the anesthesiologist,* I joked. *Getting some uninterrupted sleep where no one can find me sounds pretty good right now,* I said.

> *You have a warped sense of humor,* he said trying not to laugh too hard, *but I can't argue this time.*

> *Take care of yourself and don't take any work calls,* I joked before hanging up. *You do the same,* he replied. *Sweet dreams.*

Lucky for me, I didn't have cancer.

A COLD HARD REALITY

On the day of surgery, my close friend and client Chris flew in to help Sid take care of me and the kids while I recovered.

Sid had driving to do, and I wasn't supposed to be alone. I said no to her offer to come but I'm glad she didn't listen. It turns out, sometimes even warriors need help or a safe shoulder.

The prosecutor, the government agents, a few of my close colleagues, and some clients called or sent notes to check in.

The interesting thing I noticed, however, was the radio silence from Big Law leadership. With a few exceptions, other than very close peer colleagues, the Big Law machine didn't check in to see how I was or whether there was anything they could do to offer support or help.

Well, one left a voicemail. But only after I mentioned my observations to a buddy of his. Big Law business wasn't always compatible with compassion.

Ten days later, I was back on travel as the clock began ticking again. Like a time bomb waiting to explode.

Shortly after, it was compensation time, that tense month at the year's end when people find out whether they are a favored child or a sad disappointment.

When my phone pinged from the bottom of my purse at a New York airport on a cold winter afternoon, I knew what it was. After fumbling to find my phone, I saw the notification.

A prerecorded voicemail to my Outlook email. Not a real phone call. Not a meeting. Not even a memo.

The message was from a leader, a nice guy, who sounded like he was reading a script.

We are thrilled with your performance this year. Your hours were great. You delivered strong revenue. You kept a lot of people busy. We appreciate your hard work, he said.

Clearing his throat, he reported a small raise and a decent bonus (subject to claw-back, of course, if I left the firm in 2020).

Then, a tone-deaf closing . . .

We look forward to seeing you do it again next year.

CHAPTER 7

The Frog in the Pot

I stood on the renowned summit of the Big Law mountain supremely frustrated. The weather was dark and stormy. Not bright and sunny like I had imagined.

A prerecorded voicemail? A lame script? How impersonal can they get?

After over twenty years and three Big Law firms, I wasn't even sure they were run by humans anymore. Or maybe they didn't think humans worked there? Or they just didn't care?

There was no empathy. No real appreciation. A simple: *Are you okay? Is your family okay?* There was definitely no action or intention to offer real and sustainable support.

How did we get so cold and impersonal? How could a career that mattered become so transactional?

In the Big Law machine, it seemed okay to push women to the max, make unkept promises, undercut us when convenient, use us as poster children for diversity but not share seats at tables, or money or power . . . or offer support when any normal person would need it.

Even then, Big Law couldn't make up its mind whether it was comfortable having us in the room, whether we needed to be strong or weak, assertive or meek, candid or demure.

Maybe that's how the game is played. Maybe that's the point.

The winds howled stronger. Clouds swirled. Standing on that mountain, I screamed to the universe.

Who do they want me to be? How much more do they want before they deliver their end of the deal?

CONFLICTED

Big Law careers are tough for everyone—men and women. The experience is *materially different and more grueling* for women, especially career moms. This is where writing this book became the hardest. I didn't want to write about it.

It was easier to blame nameless, faceless Big Law leadership hidden behind a thick, dark curtain in a far-away conference room. It was infinitely harder to address complexities about challenges closer to home, among leaders, peers, colleagues, and clients, many of whom I admired professionally and liked personally.

By 2020, I was deeply conflicted. I'd worked incredibly hard. I didn't know if I could stay in Big Law for another decade, but I wasn't quite ready to give up.

I'd gotten used to the grueling climb up a greasy pole. I'd proven it was doable, even against tough odds. Aware of salary and power inequities, I navigated them. If I could close gaps and find opportunities to share power, maybe my sacrifices might make the climb easier for others.

Yet, even as I gripped that greasy pole, I wished some brave soul would finally talk about it. The rules and requirements women must live by that don't apply to men. The hard things women must do to succeed. The lonely climb up and the even lonelier existence in the upper tiers where the micro-aggressions, stereotypes, biases, and uneven competition get tougher by multiples.

I rationalized, or grudgingly accepted, many things. By the end of 2019 though, I found some challenges harder to accept.

I hated how women still had to fight to stay in a game where they weren't always fully welcome or valued. I hated being ignored, invisible, and disrespected. I didn't like the lack of empathy, camaraderie, and community.

I hated being treated like a cog in a machine where prerecorded voicemails were now the preferred method of communication. A cog used to make Big Law "look good," yet whose true and only value was billing time and collecting dollars.

I hated how men used power to undercut women peers to perpetuate unequal systems that assured our climb was harder and, then, as we got higher, how the unevenness translated to even greater challenges.

I hated feeling like I couldn't be a girl who was vulnerable. Someone who needed more humanity, respect, and dignity from a career that demanded so much from her.

I hated that I couldn't be me. Yet, the truth was, I'd been wearing so many costumes to accommodate so many people for so long, I wasn't sure who "me" was anymore.

POWER GAMES

My line of work is not for the faint of heart. Nor is it for those weak of strength and spirit. People pay me to be tough, unflappable, shrewd, and strategic. They hire me to solve very hard problems, keep them out of harm's way, and keep their reputations intact.

This is a part of the game I signed up for, the part of the game I accept.

What I didn't sign up for were all the other unspoken requirements applied to women that men aren't burdened with. The requirements that no one wants to see or say or acknowledge or change, because they are uncomfortable and inconvenient.

Women must be:

- Tough without being a bitch
- Assertive without being aggressive
- Different without being too much of an outsider
- Empathetic and approachable without being a pushover
- Direct without being offensive
- Impenetrable but "nice"
- Open to second-guessing without being defensive
- Ready to clean up the mess without taking credit

We must slay the dragons that others make angry while smiling softly and demurely to those who might find us scary or intimidating or smarter or better. And then, we must make excuses or accept criticism for demanding the same level of excellence from others that Big Law expected of us.

THE STORY OF ROB

My partner and a senior male leader named Rob (not his real name) came to see me one day after a male associate complained about "feedback" I had given. Instead of speaking with me, the associate sought out my partner.

Rob commiserated with the associate. He agreed that it can be hard to work for a "strong, assertive woman," especially when she is "under stress."

> *Geez Rob, did you ask to see the associate's work product? Did you ask him whether it was any good or if the information he provided was accurate?* I asked politely.

No.

Did you ask the associate what he thought he could do better? I asked.

No.

Did you tell him to come see me and talk about the work or the feedback? I asked.

No.

Did you tell the associate that I'm an important partner in the firm, that this is an important client of the firm, and it's important that the associate deliver the best possible work product? I asked.

No.

Instead of treating me like a valued partner who was important to our firm, Rob played into the gender card. His knee-jerk reaction was to buddy up with the associate and assume the problem was me, not the work of the associate.

Yet, both Rob and the associate knew full well the analyses we prepare often have serious repercussions for people in criminal cases. Employees often face the scrutiny of their company employer and government prosecutors. It was critical the associate get the facts and analyses right or ask for help if he struggled. He did neither.

I am unapologetically careful, even exacting, when it comes to this kind of work. It's how I protect clients. It's how I would want someone to handle my legal problem. It's why I get hired.

Rob's reaction was an ongoing problem for me and other women in Big Law.

It wasn't uncommon for our male partners to play into gender biases and undercut us. Even if they didn't mean it or realize it.

The sad truth was that I couldn't always rely on my partners to offer the same professional courtesies and support I would offer them—or that they might offer their male peers.

Worse, I couldn't rely on anyone to call them out on it.

At least he didn't tell you to smile more often when you give candid feedback, a friend joked.

THE STORY OF JERRY

It was a high-stakes meeting to talk strategy, a pivotal point in cases where clients must decide how they want to fight.

I thought you were tougher than that, a male partner from another firm said. *Are you afraid to make a hard argument to shut down the criminal case? Or is it that you just don't understand the argument? I can re-explain it if you like. . . .*

The rest of the men on the call were silent, including senior client executives and my own partners. You could have heard a pin drop.

Well, Jerry, it sounds like the problem here is that I disagree with you, I said. *If we make that argument, this prosecutor will leave the table. We should be careful not to make arguments we can't prove with hard evidence and facts. Otherwise, we'll lose credibility.*

Jerry (not his real name) hated that I was leading this case, even though his specialty was in civil cases and bank transactions. I welcomed working with others and being challenged to find the best strategies. I don't like sneaky and petty.

To deflect the discussion back to the purpose of our call, I continued, *Ultimately, Jerry, the strategy decision is up to the client. Why don't we get their thoughts?*

I'd usually get calls with apologies from senior client leaders or male peers after a call like this. There were times I offered to quit or step back. If the client believed this guy and his argument could make a criminal case magically go away, they absolutely should hire him to stand before the prosecutorial firing squad and make his pitch.

These are the kind of experiences women encounter regularly. Not just with the opposition. But also with men who are supposed to be on the same side. The hardest reality?

Realizing that others weren't willing to call those guys out and shut it down.

SID'S INSIGHTS

How is it that I can so easily be accused of being too tough and then not tough enough in the same day? And why do they always resort to shading it with gender? I wondered.

You know those comments aren't directed at you, my husband Sid said one day raising an eyebrow.

He continued, *Yes, it's demeaning. But the comments weren't about that. They were a subtle message, a dog-whistle, meant for the other guys in the room. That's the audience. If Rob, Jerry, and the associate show that you are weaker or less capable, they become stronger and wiser. It's all about establishing dominance and power. Silence or no reaction is tacit approval of the hierarchy that they are good to go.*

As I looked at the pile of examples in the context of power, Sid was right.

The associate didn't go to Rob for advice. He sought approval and agreement from a male partner that I and my women peers were hard to work for—especially when "stressed." That way, he didn't have to own that his crappy work product was, in fact, crappy.

Jerry wasn't looking to persuade me that his argument was the right tactical move or legally sound. He wanted to persuade the other guys that I wasn't tough enough to protect them. If I was weaker and dumber, he was stronger and smarter.

It changed my perspective on those interactions. Not just about guys like Rob, Jerry, and the associate, but also the audience in the room or on the phone.

If the guys in the audience won't man-up and shut that stuff down, they shouldn't have the privilege of women staying in the room or joining them at a table.

And the leaders of all these guys?

It made me realize that, if leaders want to keep women engaged, they need to care more about the environment and the culture they are perpetuating.

> If cultures force women to pretend, carry extra-heavy loads, or accept systems that don't support them, leaders shouldn't be so surprised when women leave.

I wasn't asking for anyone to fight my battles nor give me any special treatment.

In the words of Supreme Court Justice Ruth Bader Ginsberg in the documentary *RGB*,

I ask no favor for my sex. All I ask of our brethren is that they take their feet off our necks.

CAN WE NAME THESE PROBLEMS?

In her podcast, *We Can Do Hard Things*, best-selling author Glennon Doyle and her sister and business manager, Amanda, recently talked about the value and power of acknowledging and naming hard, shared problems. *"Knowing we all have this problem makes it not our problem,"* said Amanda (Doyle, Sister Act, 2021). I loved that concept.

Why is it that that law firms whose lawyers fight for fair treatment of clients have internal systems that don't fully support equality? I asked Amanda, also a former Big Law lawyer and gender studies graduate.

I was determined to understand if any organization does it well. The irony of the Big Law contradiction was maddening.

There are so many layers and challenges that come with our experience. Like the system needs us to be assertive to do our jobs, yet people in the system are not always okay with women being assertive, I lamented.

No stranger to challenges in Big Law and in business, Amanda agreed the world receives women differently and is rife with double standards and extra burdens for women. She affirmed that what I felt was real. More importantly, I wasn't alone.

In fact, Amanda recently shared in another episode that gender created a tougher environment than she imagined—not just in law but the business world (Doyle, Playing Our Roles, 2021).

> *In driving business objectives,* said Amanda, *I give people the respect of speaking directly.*

> But she shared candidly, *I'm constantly walking this tightrope of remaining as I need to be to reach the goal, but also doing this job that men never have to do, which is circling back to all of our team and partners and everyone to manage everyone's feelings. It's exhausting.*

> *Everything a woman does is received as a woman,* she explained. *Unlike a man, women don't just get to just do their jobs or be themselves. Instead, women must worry about everyone else. And then, when women who must work harder to reach head tables challenge mediocrity, people judge them as "perfectionists," or "overbearing," or "demanding."*

Amanda's observations hit home. They sharpened some thoughts on my own experiences.

A woman not only has to be excellent and watch out for everyone's feelings. She also must watch out for those who affirmatively use her gender to undermine her and assert power over her—overtly, subtlety, and even from behind the scenes.

What Big Law leadership and male peers failed to understand is that these were among the insidious systemic challenges that make the climb infinitely longer and more arduous for women. No one talks about it because no one wants to see or acknowledge it. But it's there. Every moment of every day.

By the time women reach the upper tiers of Big Law, we've already shouldered years of managing many more jobs and roles then anyone wants to acknowledge in a crushing, unsupportive environment. And then, we must find ways to sustain in yet another elite male-dominated world. It becomes that much harder.

PERSPECTIVE AND ACCOUNTABILITY

I'm not arguing that the problem lays with all men or that I don't like my male colleagues.

I like and admire many men I've worked with over time, including those with more power than me. Nevertheless, at times, I thought they were clueless or tone-deaf or vision impaired or even hypocritical. There were jerks, of course, but I had plenty of eye-roll moments among colleagues I respected.

> I saw too many instances where no one spoke up in the face of barriers to equality, microaggressions, or comments clearly rooted in gender biases. Lack of support made me question the integrity and courage of everyone in the room and in the system.

I saw too many instances where women didn't always feel part of the team, in the same foxhole or, at times, even on the same planet.

I was continuously surprised by male colleagues who claimed they had no power to equalize systemic challenges. Yet, they were paid bigger dollars, bestowed titles, and had chairs at every meeting that mattered. The system seemed to work quite well for them yet balancing the scales more evenly seemed beyond their abilities.

From my legal work in corporate ethics and investigations, I know that culture is greatly impacted by those at the top—those with titles, seats, power, and money.

In a profession that is rooted in fighting for justice, fairness, and equality, I wanted to know how we justice seekers and justice defenders, of all people, didn't practice what we preached.

Was anyone really looking out for the greater good?

In 2020, in my spare time, I began studying leadership. Not just from the perspective of what makes a leader good or bad, but how leaders influence culture. I wanted to find secrets that could help me solve my problem. A problem I perceived must be rooted in crummy leadership.

That's how I met Gary Heil.

That is how my world began slowly turning right side up.

Gary was the perfect muse. Brilliant, witty, and charming, yet equal parts frustrating and annoying. He was a combination of my dad and my old boss Bill. His seemingly encyclopedic knowledge of behavioral research and studies on human psychology made it hard to argue with him, like a competitive sport, both invigorating and exhausting.

Over many months, Gary talked about research on human motivation. He regaled me with stories of the teachings of Austrian neurologist and Holocaust survivor Viktor Frankl and famed psychologist Abraham Maslow and his "hierarchy of needs." Gary pushed me to look not just at leaders, but the entire ecosystem of leadership and culture. That meant everyone, including me.

He wondered if I had the courage to stare at myself in the mirror and own my own choices?

Our conversations went something like this:

> Me: *Leaders stink at leading. They have all the power. I can't understand why they can't fix problems that are so obvious?*

> Gary: *You know it's not that simple. You're seeking a culture shift. Yet humans by nature are negative, pessimistic, and stuck in their ways. We like predictable, stable systems. Change creates fear and uncertainty, especially when we're talking about redistributing power and money. The top can't create change alone.*

Me: *We just need more people like me who are willing to buck the system from within. Partner with leaders who want change.*

Gary (laughing): *Let me ask you something. You've said that many lawyers are unhappy with the law firm model. If that's true, and I believe you, why haven't they changed it? And, if they can't change it, why do they stay?*

Gary: *They stay because the system is familiar, even acceptable to them. They decide the incentives are worth trade-offs. Now you are talking about changing those trade-offs. For everyone. So, I have to ask this question, why do you stay?*

Gary understood why I was focused on the pyramid's peak. He continued to hammer home leadership's complex layers, emphasizing the roles of my partners and me in the leadership ecosystem. Leadership, he argued, doesn't just live at the top of an organization. It never will.

If leaders could not equalize the system, it could be because many of us accepted the imbalanced scales as they were—even if grudgingly.

Maybe we all carry some responsibility. Maybe that's partly why we don't speak up.

THE FROG IN THE POT

On a rare peaceful afternoon, I was savoring a perfect cup of coffee in my comfortable kitchen chair. The smell of coffee grounds and hazelnut permeated the air. The kids were in camp. Our two dogs napped peacefully by my feet.

When my phone rang, Gary's name popped up. Curious about his latest musings, I answered.

Gary had tried for months to convince me about culture's impact on human behavior, and human behavior's impact on culture.

Groups inherently wield a lot of power on their own, he'd say.

Perhaps I needed to consider incentives that create warped cultures, and the possibility that leaders and groups don't see toxic cultures creep up over time until it's too late. When little paper cuts become deeper wounds.

As he often does to illustrate a point, Gary shared a story.

It was the old fable about a frog in the pot. The frog relaxes in refreshing water. A known environment. He's comfortable.

Over time, the water warms little by little. Unaware of the danger, the frog slowly cooks to death.

As Gary reached the story's crescendo, he started laughing.

You know that story's complete bullshit, right? he exclaimed. *The frog's survival instincts will actually tell him to jump out.*

So, are you saying I'm like the frog in the metaphor? I asked.

No, he said, *Sadly, it's worse. The frog gets out.*

And I stayed, I said softly.

Exactly, said Gary.

Horrified and amused, I laughed at the visual.

There I am, hanging out on half a lily pad, treading in a Big Law pot of water with my big bag of boulders. The temperature is rising ever so slowly.

Sitting on a spoon, a frog looks at me quizzically from the outside. His big eyes are pleading with me to save myself.

Yet, I stay as the water begins to boil.

Stubborn to a fault. Still determined to prove this girl could tough it out and tread water just like the men.

But the guys aren't even on the greasy pole or in the pot, the frog whispered, his big eyes blinking.

They took the elevator. And I hate to tell you this. None of them are carrying all those boulders.

CHAPTER 8

Big Law's Final Act

By early 2021, to say I wasn't doing well is an understatement. Years of "doing it all" had taken their toll. Yet, it was the Big Law culture and trying to play catch up to beat the gender odds that delivered the toughest blows.

Alone in my pot, the bubbles rising, temperature increasing. I wondered what happened to the girl who came to Washington and the warrior she became.

Once impenetrable, the tattered layers of my warrior suit were dirty and ragged. The skeleton of the steel frame visibly bent. Heavy and bulky, it dragged me deeper into the water.

Wounded, broken, and sad, I called my friend Danny. A former prosecutor like me, we had worked some of the same defense-side cases for years.

I can't do it anymore, Danny, I said trying to keep it together. *I've done everything they asked. I've been the good soldier. I have nothing left to give. I need to ask you for a favor . . .*

Before I could finish my sentence, Danny said, *Name it.*

My out loud admission to a long-time friend that I could no longer "do it all" allowed me to breathe. Something I hadn't been able to do for a while.

THE COST OF THE HAMSTER WHEEL

2020 had its own share of battles that compounded further the fractures in my armor, exposing deeper wounds.

- Tackling new, complex client challenges

- Working with my siblings to empty and sell our childhood home and finishing my parents' relocation to a community with long-term care for our dad

- Navigating a pandemic that changed life as we knew it, increasing isolation, shifting to a strange virtual life

- Shielding Olivia who battled daggers of middle school girl meanness, age-old weapons that wound deeply, now online for the world to see

- Throwing myself into leadership studies in an attempt to understand leadership gaps and culture challenges that were crushing people like me

- More voicemails, even fewer personal touches in a world where this warrior felt more isolated yet exposed

As winter approached, my shoulder was killing me, my daughter was in crisis, and clients were stressed under the weight and pressures of mounting problems. In October 2020 alone, I billed almost one hundred hours per week from my dining room, averaging twelve hours a day, seven days a week.

No breaks. Same story. Different day. Twenty plus years.

And the worst?

Realizing that when I asked for Big Law support on important revenue-generating work, like an actual understanding of resources needed or proper coordination on key client matters and internal politics, I was offered only bromides. To my male-dominated leadership—no matter the firm, no matter the money involved—I was worth no more than expensive bottles of booze, email platitudes, and the very clear message that I was to suck it up.

After all, I was—always and forever—someone's bitch. No matter how high in the tier-structure I climbed. No matter how hard I worked. No matter what rickety table or half a chair I sat in. No matter how many flags I or my female colleagues waved nor how convenient we made it for our male colleagues to accept our presence. No matter how much we tried to ignore or forgive all the indignities that came with making a longer, more arduous climb.

In hindsight, I guess it always felt that way. Yet, somehow, hearing those words out loud, stark, cold, and blunt was something else entirely.

THE MONEY GAME AND THE HAMSTER WHEEL

By December, wiped out and bloody from the battles that raged, the irony didn't escape me that I had a date with another anesthesiologist. This time, I wasn't looking forward to it.

In weeks leading up to surgery, I made sure cases transferred to other lawyers, coordinated with clients, and developed clear strategies to assure seamless transitions. The time stamp on my last email before leaving for my 6:00 a.m. surgery check-in was 4:30 a.m., January 5, 2021, the day before Jack's twelfth birthday.

I was warned shoulder surgery would be difficult. Yet, as I woke up in a deep fog of drugs, numbness, tingling, and pain, I learned it was worse than predicted.

With repairs to my labrum and rotator cuff, the relocation of my bicep tendon, and multiple screws that created stress fractures in my bones, the surgeon said it was like four surgeries in one. A long and painful recovery lay ahead. Now, instead of a boiling pot, I was packed in an ice machine.

Weeks later, I'd face some of the toughest decisions of my career. Even if I could physically and mentally return to the Big Law game and start over, the question was whether I should. And if I didn't, what my future would look like.

By February 2021, after talking with Danny, I knew I had a lifeline if I decided to take it.

That was important. Although larger cases and clients were now being handled by others, there were a few matters that I couldn't hand-off, like a Special Counsel position that wasn't transferrable.

I'm not asking for anything fancy, I told Danny on that cold winter day. *I don't care about money. If I make a change, I just need to make sure the non-transferrable clients are handled. I need a home until I can really get back on my feet.*

Danny's firm gave me an important option if I decided to leave Big Law. A decision I didn't take lightly.

It meant walking away from the seven-figure salary I'd fought so hard for, the greasy pole I'd clung to, the familiar yet horrid chains of the hamster wheel in the rickety cage that had been my home. The predictable and familiar. The devil I knew.

Now, I waited on the money game.

In Big Law, firms pay most of an equity partner's salary at the firm's "year-end."

Salaries like mine were distributed in pieces during the year with a big chunk later. That last payment is based on shares allotted to the partner multiplied by the share value, a number that varies depending on firm revenue collected.

For an equity partner, the money game concludes after the books close, the king's council announces share values and bonuses, and the money is in your bank account.

In late February 2021, a generic firm-wide voicemail and a memo informed me that I got a raise for the next year and a bonus (subject to claw-back if I left within a year), a signal I was still a favored child.

By March, the distribution of salaries and bonuses complete, I needed to decide. I knew the right answer. I just wasn't looking forward to it.

Leaving Big Law firms is never pleasant.

Like any divorce, there can be bad feelings when someone leaves the family. The amount of hurt and blowback depends on who takes what property (clients) and inevitable slights felt on either side.

Having been through this a few times, I'd jokingly warn peers who made law firm moves that it's important to maintain perspective and distance. They shouldn't expect their former leaders, colleagues, and friends to be loyal, polite, or friendly.

Transitions are tough. Business is business. Cash is king.

But I told myself my situation was different. Unlike others who moved to Big Law competitor firms, I was a wounded warrior mom stepping back. I wasn't taking anyone's clients. Key transitions already were made prior to my surgery. We had no major uncertainties about property. I wasn't even getting back on the field for a while.

To make our divorce pleasant, I attributed my departure to shoulder surgery and the needs of my family.

The party line I practiced and repeated for Big Law leadership went something like this:

> *I'm retiring from Big Law. I'm exhausted, burned out, injured. I need to heal. I've left everything on the field for Big Law. I'm not going to a competitor. I'm going to a small firm with long-time friends. I won't be working at the same pace. I'm shifting priorities and walking away from a big salary to focus more on being a mom. It's a life change, a family decision. It's nothing personal. Nothing against you.*

While the party line had many elements of truth, it didn't offer the complete picture.

By now and with good reason, I didn't think anyone would care about it. After decades in the industry, I knew from experience Big Law didn't pay real attention to the myriad layers of challenges women face, nor the reasons behind my burnout. That includes every firm I'd been affiliated with. I heard similar complaints from warrior friends at other firms.

I was willing to shade the truth to keep my departure cordial, comfortable, convenient.

Why? Speaking out wasn't worth it. I had a lot of money at stake.

Hundreds of thousands of dollars in bonus and capital, that huge wad of money equity partners are required to "invest" in the partnership.

I had the bonus in my pocket. Big Law had the capital and a lot of power.

What I wanted was simple:

> An expedited, uncontested, friendly divorce or "conscious uncoupling" famous people like Gwyneth Paltrow get.
>
> Retention of money I legitimately earned.
>
> Expedited return of my personal investment.

I wanted to be gracious and, in return, get some needed, expedited financial breathing room to re-allocate investments and refinance our home mortgage to accommodate the loss of my salary.

Given my circumstances, you would think the requests would be a no-brainer, especially for a senior-level woman who was leaving due to matters of health and taking care of children she'd neglected for years in the name of Big Law and its clients.

But I wouldn't get off that easy.

At least not without a few final, below-the-belt blows by Big Law and minions of the king's secret council. They had the power. It seemed important to them to make sure I knew it.

THE DECISION

It was Monday, March 8, 2021.

International Women's Day. A day that celebrates women's achievements. I was choosing freedom.

The night before, I sent the firm leadership an email asking to speak about some difficult decisions I'd made. It was time for me to explain.

The initial call went as well as could be expected. Better actually.

Leadership was understanding, even sympathetic. My law firm was sad to lose me, they said. They asked me to consider an alternative.

> We'd like to offer you the same lifeline your friend gave you. Is there a possibility you would consider going on leave? Take a sabbatical or more time to think about the decision? We could talk in a month, two months, or six months. Whenever works for you. Don't make any rash decisions. When you feel better, you can get back on the playing field just like before.

I listened closely, even after the call was long over.

What was missing were things like this:

We know you've reached out about support. We're sorry you haven't gotten it.

We don't want to lose a strong woman like you. What do you think caused the burnout? What could we have done to help? Is there anything we can do now?

What can we do to avoid losing other women like you?

We'll make sure the playing field looks different. We care about your health and well-being. Above all, we want you to feel valued.

We're sorry. We should have done better.

What I heard instead was this:

Big Law was willing to have me take a break to get back on the same field. The one I'd played for years at a deficit, yet still delivered strong results. The one where my work family wasn't always supportive and, at times, handicapped women like me. The one where I had to pretend.

Even with studies, articles, social media posts, and journals being published daily about the ongoing exodus of career women, my firm and Big Law, the industry, still didn't get it.

Shortly after, I shared my conversation with Sid, Jack, and Olivia in our kitchen. Emotionally spent, I was at a crossroads, a point of no return. Trying to be supportive, Sid and Jack dutifully listened but they were done.

Olivia left the room without saying a word.

MONEY OR HAPPINESS?

Later that afternoon, I drove Olivia to her volleyball practice. It was clear and chilly. Country music played softly on the radio.

Olivia seemed quiet, as if processing her thoughts. After a few minutes of silence and not one to mince words, she asked:

So, what's it gonna be, Mom? Money or happiness?

Surprised, I said,

That's an interesting way to put it. Want to tell me what you really think?

As we waited at a traffic light, she turned to face me:

Well, isn't that the question you would ask me? Do you want to stay stuck in a world where you don't feel valued? Or are you willing to take a chance and be open to more? Change can bring great opportunities.

I hate it when my kids use my words against me.

When I shared with Sid what Olivia said, he laughed, then offered observations of his own.

> *You realize we've been to this dance before, right? Law firms make promises they don't keep. You try to make things better, take courses, hire coaches, meet great leaders for advice. You don't want to fail. Then, you get a head injury from banging your head against that same wall.*
>
> *Walking away from your paycheck is a big deal. But none of the stuff we have matters if we don't have you.*
>
> *It might be time for you to consider whether Big Law is set up exactly how they want it to be. And whether you are on a hamster wheel because they have no intention of treating you equally.*
>
> *The question may be this. Who do you want to be going forward?"*

What Sid said wasn't an unreasonable observation. As I ruminated overnight, Olivia's and Sid's words played in my head.

The next day, I drafted an email to Big Law leadership.

I thanked them for the opportunity and alternative they offered. I politely declined and set forth my requests based on the material changes in our family's financial position.

Then, I pressed send.

In light of the personal challenges I had been facing, I hung on to that sliver of hope that Big Law would do the right thing.

Not just *use* the word "family," but perhaps live it.

It was not to be. Apropos of the greasy pole phone call where it all began, leadership returned a nice note confirming our friendship, then disappeared.

BIG LAW'S FINAL ACT

Can we say you are only working part-time? How few hours?

Can we say you don't plan to go to a Big Law competitor firm any time soon? Or ever?

Will your new firm issue a press release? Um, because it might be a problem if someone announces you are actually working there. . . .

Having explained my medical challenges, I wondered if the next question would be if I could stop breathing for a while.

It wasn't enough for Big Law that I was a broken and burned-out warrior career mom. The system wanted to make sure the warrior was no longer a warrior nor able to fight. In other words, that I would not rise up and be competition. (Which was sort of a joke given my physical condition at the time. Raising a sword was definitely out of the question.)

Hovering like demons by the door holding the key, they wanted her to hand over her tattered armor, her identity, and sign in blood on the sword at the foot of the king's secret council that she was no longer a warrior (or at least she'd stay down there for a while). Then, it seemed important that she remain publicly demure so as not to draw the ire of the king's secret council who still wielded the power to make her life difficult.

To be honest, their requests seemed excessive.

I wasn't asking for more than what they deemed I'd earned. While a male friend in Big Law questioned whether certain of their demands were enforceable, at that point, I didn't care. They could have the armor. It was a mess anyway. My identity and my dignity, however, were not for sale.

It didn't end there.

When it came to the return of my capital, the Big Law minions demanded that I collect invoices from a long-time firm client that belonged to firm leadership. (So, on the one hand they wanted me to stay down and hand over the armor. On the other hand, the minions figured I could clean up a few administrative tasks on my way out for firm leaders who were apparently too busy to do it themselves.)

If you are WONDERING, I never got questions about what Big Law could have done better to keep me or other women like me.

But that wasn't unusual in my experience. The Big Law industry never asks.

And, while I know some worked behind the scenes on my behalf, leadership remained silent. As with "the families" I'd been part of in the past, those behind dark curtains never showed their faces nor spoke directly to me.

So much for being a valued family member.

Would the system have treated a male soldier differently, some have asked? Great question. Based on the societal biases that crawled out of the woodwork when my husband changed roles and the favoritism evident in Big Law, I have no doubt. A male soldier, even a healthy one, would be honored, celebrated, revered for leaving to take care of his kids.

I could only imagine the experience for a man among the inner circle.

THE TURNING POINT BEGINS

Leaving Big Law was one thing. Learning how to live beyond Big Law was another.

In the months ahead, I wrote a leadership book that lacked depth in personal stories. I nursed my health. I graduated from middle school a second time (or it sure felt like it). Just when it seemed the summer sun was here, my health suffered a setback that required a full-scale stop of activities. Nerve and muscular issues were apparent side effects from the trauma of surgery and the slow recovery afterward.

I had to sit with myself. Sometimes in dark rooms to break the cycle of headaches. Do nothing. For over a month. It was like being in a dark interrogation room sitting upright in an ergonomic plastic chair for days on end.

I hate plastic chairs. I hate doing nothing even more. In fact, I suck at it.

Around the same time, the woman career coach published ill-fated advice suggesting:

> Working moms fail to reach their potential because we aren't paying enough attention to upward mobility.

> We lack focus. We're over-burdened.

> We don't have lunches with colleagues, take on enough business development roles, or join social events after work.

> It's our fault. We need to work harder. Show more commitment.

Backlash from working moms and women lawyers was swift and harsh. Warrior career moms wrote posts detailing everything they juggle to make it all work and deliver excellence. I wanted to gently tell them to take a break.

Several people who knew my story reached out, encouraging me to write a response. Still reluctant, I watched responses online for days. Interestingly, I didn't see anything from Big Law leadership.

Dipping my toe in the water, fearing judgment and criticism, I agonized over my carefully crafted LinkedIn article full of disclaimers.

Women Don't Need to Work Harder. The Legal Profession Needs to Change: My Response to the ABA Journal Article 'Are Women Paying Enough Attention to Upward Mobility?' marked the beginning of my real turning point.

At the time, I couldn't have predicted the reactions I'd receive, not just from women in Big Law or the legal profession but across industries.

Women were more hurt, sad, angry, ashamed, and filled with feelings of devaluation in ways I'd never imagined.

Many women felt they couldn't speak up.

They didn't want to hurt feelings of male peers or leaders or referral networks.

They didn't want to sound angry, bitter, ungrateful. They didn't want to be the target of judgment or criticism.

They were tired of repeating themselves. They didn't think anyone believed what women experience.

They didn't think their story was "bad enough," like a horrible front page news story.

They didn't want to criticize a system they benefitted from, even if support they received was less than their male peers.

They wanted change, but they didn't believe their voice would make a difference.

We're sure glad someone is willing to say it though, they said. *We're glad someone is naming the problem.*

And so began my true redemption.

* * *

Redemption begins with facing difficult truths.

The ones most people are afraid to face. Even me.

It is time for me to speak my truth about why I left Big Law. About how Burnout came calling.

And the nitty gritty of why senior women leave their jobs, and the reason why leaders lose them.

While we're at it, let's also look at why women opt-out and build their own tables.

Yes, I'm afraid. I'm human. I'm vulnerable.

But I am a warrior. I will tell you the truth.

PART III

TURNING POINT

*A woman is like a tea bag. You never know
how strong she is until she gets in hot water.*

—ELEANOR ROOSEVELT

*When a woman rises up in glory, her energy is
magnetic and her sense of possibility contagious.*

—MARIANNE WILLIAMSON

CHAPTER 9

The Truth

No one wants to talk about their *true* reflection in the mirror. Not the pretty one that has been air brushed to perfection. The one that exposes imperfections, blemishes, and age. The stuff we hope no one sees.

We have a choice. To look or not to look.

When Olivia asked the question *"money or happiness"* that day, she made clear I wasn't being a very good role model. Perhaps even a tad hypocritical. I wasn't walking my talk.

Looking at the "young me" in her face, I knew it too.

My frustrations with Big Law went beyond the unrelenting pace of the work. It was the uneven game, the ruse, and serving a system that tolerates and perpetuates the unequal treatment of women. Where business is business, cash is king.

I just wanted someone to admit it. If the Big Law system and its leaders aren't willing to drive change, we should stop using fake words like "partner," "family," "friend," or "diversity and inclusion" when no one really means it. Say what the system is. Have the courage to be who you are.

Stop making women take on extra work and added burdens that don't support the *true mission*. Don't play bait and switch with seats and tables. Don't saddle us with programs that were never intended to succeed. That just sets us up for never-ending failure and makes us question our success and work ethic.

Being honest means everyone can reassess the value of the relationship too, with eyes wide open. No false expectations. It has the added value of giving women precious time back to focus on what matters most—like building books of business, taking a nap, or spending time with our kids.

In the face of my daughter calling me out, I realized that I was at an important crossroads. I had a choice. Stay or leave?

If I chose to stay in Big Law, no matter the firm—for me—it meant acceptance of the greasy pole climb. It meant that I was okay with the ruse, the "bitch story," and a system that didn't value me equally. That I was okay with it all.

Then, I'd have to explain my rationale to my ever-perceptive daughter, Olivia. The same girl I'd been lecturing to about living life without regrets, embracing change, having the courage to stand up for herself, and not being afraid to speak out.

I could only *imagine* what she'd say.

TAKING MY OWN MEDICINE

That night, after getting home from volleyball practice with Olivia and talking with Sid, I went back to my leadership research to find inspiration and wisdom.

I wanted to remember what it felt like to be the girl who came to Washington, who believed the only barriers were the ones in her mind. The one who threw that career counsellor's silly list in the trash because it didn't measure up to her dreams.

I wanted to find myself. Not the warrior. Me.

Among the quotes I poured over that now hang on my office bulletin board were ones from people who shared thoughts with me on my leadership journey about walking the walk, living without regret, and not fearing failure.

Leadership isn't something you learn in a classroom. It's about learning who you are, challenging yourself, being curious. Above all, you must be sure to not only talk the talk but walk the walk.
—RETIRED BRIGADIER GENERAL DANA BORN, FIRST WOMAN DEAN OF STUDENTS, US AIR FORCE ACADEMY, LECTURER AT THE HARVARD KENNEDY SCHOOL OF GOVERNMENT

I am grateful for the life I have. I want to inspire people to see their lives differently. To live life on their own terms, without regret.
—CHRIS KOCH, FARMER AND MOTIVATIONAL SPEAKER FEATURED ON OPRAH'S SUPER SOUL SUNDAY. BORN WITH NO ARMS AND NO LEGS, CHRIS DROVE A COMBINE TRACTOR IN CANADA AS WE TALKED BY PHONE.

The impossible exists in our mindset, which is why we must get out of our habits, certitudes, and beliefs that keep us prisoners of old ways of thinking. Adventure and exploration is not anymore about discovering new territories, but about making this planet a better place to live. We should not be afraid. The only way to never fail is to never try.
—DR. BERTRAND PICCARD, SWISS PSYCHIATRIST, BALLOONIST, HUMANITARIAN; CO-PILOT OF THE FIRST AROUND THE WORLD NONSTOP BALLOON FLIGHT AND THE FIRST SOLAR-POWERED AIRPLANE FLIGHT

As I processed the advice and stories shared by Dana, Chris, Dr. Piccard, among many others, I knew that Big Law and other male-dominated systems were not the only ones who needed to take off the veneer, "get real," and say who they are. So did I.

TOUGH REALITIES

When Olivia called me out, she wanted her mom back—the girl warrior beneath the suit. She wasn't interested in the faux suit, nor the leadership billboard of words, nor the exhausted working mom who accepted less for herself.

Not only wasn't I walking my talk, I wasn't using my investigative skills and curiosity to see the entirety of the problem. I was only conveniently scratching the surface. Perhaps out of fear or guilt or frustration.

I wanted to blame Big Law leaders for all the double standards. The system flaws. The lack of human kindness, compassion, empathy. After all, they set the tone.

But Gary Heil forced me to look at Big Law complexities differently, like I would do in an investigation. It painted an infinitely more complicated picture involving all the players in the game. Gary wasn't letting leaders off the hook, but he wasn't letting my peers or me get off scot-free either.

The herd has a lot of power, Gary would say. *Leaders can't change culture alone, even if change is sorely needed. Every day is a choice,* Gary said. *You get to decide if you want to run with the herd or forge a new path.*

This is where Nick Craig came into the picture. The person I'd been avoiding for months.

MEETING "GANDALF"

Nick is a leadership expert and best-selling author—the one who coached Brené Brown on her "purpose statement," those words that represent the meaning you bring to the world. Your unique gift, no matter your job or title.

Nick scared me not because of his impressive pedigree. It was the whole concept of "purpose." And anything having to do with vulnerability.

When I first met him, I wanted to understand how to find rare, effective leaders who actually lived and led from their purpose. How could I get past mere words and recognize them?

Purpose is a strength, Nick said. *It's not what you do. It's how you do it and why—the strengths and passions you bring to the table no matter where you're seated. You'll know these leaders by understanding this better for yourself.*

Nick shared his curiosity about stories of redemption and renewal, something that's intrigued him since he was a teen. It's become his life's work and his guiding force.

So, what is your purpose statement? I asked out loud.

To wake you up and have you find that you are home, Nick said.

The poetry version is: *I am the Gandalf that knocks on your door. If you open it, you will know the deeper truth of who you are.* (Gandalf, the wizard in J.R.R. Tolkien's novel *Lord of the Rings*, has great powers and leads by encouraging and mentoring.)

When Nick first invited me to work with him on my purpose statement, I passed. I'd do anything to avoid the "vulnerable" thing, including hiding or catching the plague.

In early 2021, I relented. Along with savvy corporate executives from Fortune 500 companies and military leaders from West Point, we examined pivotal stories in our lives that influenced how we lived and led: magical moments from childhood, crucible experiences, or a passion that fueled us.

Magical moments and passions were easier to talk about. The crucibles crushed me.

It was where I found the origins of the warrior suit and its steely, thick protective layers.

The suit initially constructed by a girl to protect against and ward off the injustices of life.

That later became the girl's source of strength and fortitude, allowing her to fight for the rights, empowerment, and voices of others.

So that others who felt weak might again feel strong, who felt threatened might have protection, or who felt invisible might be seen.

That girl was no dummy.

> She saw the chasm between the world where we fought for our clients and the world we lived in.

She felt the blows and wounds from battle that never had time to heal.

She felt the weight of the unrelenting climb, system inequities, double standards, and wounds caused by friendly fire.

She was the one bleeding below.

She was tired of the game.

Nick's world is about finding out who you are so you can truly be home.

To truly be home, I realized that I had to be willing to finally stand up for myself, and people like me, in the same way I stand up for others.

It meant saying what no one wants to hear. What so many women are afraid to say. Me included. But, this time, without my heavy, warped, bullet-laden armor. As me. Just the girl. To be an advocate in the truest sense.

THE TRUTH

Objectively, what does it say that women are still leaving Big Law in droves, at much higher rates than men, including those who fearlessly made their way into the upper ranks?

The data, studies, and reports confirm at least some reasons why. Yet, they don't and can't convey the harm unequal systems inflict on humans who live in them. Only the bloody, sweaty, messy realities women face can do that. It's why I wrote this book.

I know some will want more reassurance that women leaving jobs isn't "their fault." Unfortunately, I can't give you that.

To understand our reality, you might need to be uncomfortable in your own reflections for a bit. Or perhaps consider seeing the world through a woman's eyes, who was not a shrinking violet or a wallflower, yet had to eat her fair share of humble pie and who finally said *enough*.

The truth is: the system isn't okay.

I wasn't okay working ten times as hard or having to overcome the pileup of innumerable biases or contorting myself into a pretzel to make everyone feel better about competing with women.

I wasn't okay that the statistics about the promotion and retention of women in Big Law were only marginally better than when I became an equity partner over a decade ago.

I wasn't okay that there was so little awareness of the challenges women face throughout the climb, and the lack of honesty about why women leave.

I wasn't okay with the uneven game, the diversity ruse, nor the indignities many women must face day in and day out.

I wasn't okay being silent, pretending, or living with stark contradictions and double standards.

I've tried to break it down further here.

THE UNEVEN GAME

Big Law today is about big money. The ultimate Holy Grail is revenue, the average profits for partner, and how high we can jack up lawyer hourly rates to sustain profits. Not partnership, friendship, family, nor equality or inclusion. The Big Law business model is based on billable time, a metric that isn't all that creative and presents inherent and disproportionate challenges for women—especially working moms, even if their significant others help.

Why? Billing by finite measures of time has an inevitable cap given the number of hours in a day (twenty-four by my last count). To further increase revenue Big Law charges obscene rates per hour, which are now at levels that create hostility and distrust with clients. That doesn't help women either. (Billable hours is a metric everyone hates, by the way—lawyers and clients. I can't imagine we can't do better.)

I'm not opposed to businesses being about big money and not investing in culture. But we should all own who we are. More importantly, we should stop faking who we are not. The truth is the game as it is currently configured is uneven for women. The climb is much harder. Big Law has not invested enough to change that experience nor the attitudes that perpetuate it. In fact, the Big Law system actually incentivizes people to play the game exactly as it's configured. That is the truth.

THE DIVERSITY RUSE

Then, there's the diversity ruse.

Big Law as an industry isn't *really* struggling with equality or diversity and inclusion. As women leave in droves or decide not to join the party at all, Big Law is struggling with how to explain those numbers to maintain the ruse. To say it's not their fault.

To be seen as part of the Big Law team, women must play along. We're saddled with responsibilities that aren't designed to succeed, yet we can't publicly criticize them. We can't risk our paychecks or risk alienating leaders or peers. So, we hold our nose and cheer.

I'm not saying diversity and inclusion programs aren't valuable, or that there aren't some firms who do better than others.

But we all know that Big Law is notorious for under-investing in these programs.

Women waste precious time waving flags to support something that: isn't designed to succeed or change attitudes in the system; doesn't support the ultimate bottom line leaders value most; and doesn't materially improve their experience or their ability to sustain a greasy pole climb.

DIRTY PLAY: KNIFE WOUNDS, PAPER CUTS, CHEAP SHOTS, AND JABS

To make matters worse, the system allows other participants in the game to play dirty.

What's the difference between knife wounds, paper cuts, cheap shots, and jabs? They can be different depending on how an individual experiences them. I won't try to define them here. My "tolerances" may be different than others.

What I will say is that dirty play hurts and handicaps women even further.

For me, the systemic challenges, lack of respect for women as leaders, and perpetuation or tolerance of innumerable, deeply-rooted inequities and biases were the most damaging. They felt demoralizing, undermining, and isolating. The juvenile or boorish behaviors I shut down with greater ease. Insulting and demeaning, yes, but they could be emotionally compartmentalized or ignored.

I've described systemic challenges throughout this book to offer a window into our world. I've focused less on some of the more blatant experiences.

Here are just few more gems. I invite you, the reader, to decide how the following behaviors sit with you.

> Imagine getting called away from your work to join male colleagues who want to discuss a "business opportunity." You learn a client has a new top lawyer,

a woman they describe as "not that smart." They expect she'll "make mistakes" that will assure they can get more business. They ask you to have lunch with her, see if you can become her new best friend, and report back what you learn. It's a move that reconfirms some male partners think women clients are ripe targets for women partners to "get close to," and not because of our respective brain power or interests.

Imagine men with leadership titles who acted inappropriately: a leader who drove high performing women out of the firm without questions from management, or the one who urinated in an alley as other lawyers tried to shuffle junior lawyers away, or the one who lived in the office with a fully stocked bar and walked around half-dressed on weekends, or the one who informed a woman partner about her 50 percent pay cut and suggested her wife get a job in a year they paid themselves handsomely—or the one nicknamed a "walking lawsuit" for his notorious reputation with women yet who maintained his leadership title for years.

Imagine the supervisor her father's age who asked her out on a date, the picture of the penis emailed as "a joke," the men who couldn't stop talking about the strip bar they frequented, the men with wandering eyes.

The list goes on. . . .

The worst?

Hearing people say "it doesn't happen here" when everyone knows it does.

INABILITY TO SPEAK OUT

I don't blame women for not speaking out about system flaws.

Women who speak out aren't embraced. They get labeled as bitter or angry or aggressive or worse. Our system isn't open to feedback. Rather, the system would rather we stop "complaining," suck it up, be grateful, accept the indignities, and keep playing hard like the lower-level team members the system deems us to be.

This is perhaps the worst part. Staying silent means more than just silence or acceptance. It means living a double life, carrying extra loads quietly to make sure everyone feels better, accepting less, ignoring biases, microaggressions, and wounds. It means pretending it is all okay—when it's not.

WHY SOME WOMEN LEAVE.

Some women leave because we get tired of *all of the above*.

We get tired of a business model that forces us to choose between real family and never-ending work in an environment that doesn't truly support or embrace us. We get tired of living on a razor-thin edge, one or two crises away from that choice being forced upon us when we can't "do it all" anymore. We get tired of the demands the system places on us without the system living up to its end of the deal.

The truth is that I was no longer okay experiencing a reality our leaders and peers don't see or won't acknowledge and address.

Even if I was paid a lot of money.

I was no longer okay with the temperature of the water, greasy poles, steep endless climbs, broken promises, uneven games, and wounds. I was no longer okay accommodating.

I couldn't rationalize for my kids why I stayed in a job where I wasn't treated as an equal nor valued as the high-performing asset I was.

I realized that wounds and biases stacked up over time and finally took their toll. Even for a tough warrior like me.

In the end, no matter how much I loved some of the work, I never wanted to become so numb, cynical, or hardened that I lost my sense of pride and self-worth. Or that I became forever disconnected from my true purpose and guiding force. That's right, my mission.

To be the voice in the wind
who brings lift to your wings.

That is why I left my high-paying job in Big Law.

Yes, it was scary. Yet I felt a sense of freedom.

It was one of the saddest, most empowering days of my career.

MY REDEMPTION

While I'm far from perfect, Olivia and the girl warrior made clear that if our jobs are about advocating for justice for clients, we must be free to do the same for ourselves.

Nick asked me once whether the reason I passionate fighting for the underdog was because, in a way, I was an underdog. The answer is undoubtedly, yes.

Yet, happily, after shedding the remains of my warrior suit, I found an incredible truth.

The key to the door that would finally bring me home:

With time to heal, the girl was stronger than I'd ever imagined.

A warrior and underdog in her own right, saved yet suffocating, under the weight of a suit no longer needed. A suit that no longer fit.

To survive, she needed to be free.
By being free, she could thrive. Because
she believed in herself and her ability to fly
higher and achieve infinitely more.

* * *

Seeing my true self again reminded me of an old friend, Fred Fielding, and the sage advice he offered many years ago when I was on the cusp of moving beyond my first law firm, more than doubling my salary.

Would I be worth the investment, I wondered? *Should I believe in my ability to achieve more?*

Fred is a brilliant lawyer and strategist who served as White House counsel to Presidents Ronald Reagan and George W. Bush.

He gave me courage to believe I could do more.

Not just because I was capable of more but because I was worthy.

Taking risks to stretch beyond where you are is the type of effort the world needs to solve hard problems, he would say.

Earlier this year, Fred wrote Olivia a letter as she was considering big changes for high school. The young girl who used to sing to him by video as a toddler.

Everything came full circle.

In his letter, Fred focused on attributes that kept him grounded throughout his career—his belief in the importance of living a purpose beyond yourself.

To do what you were meant to achieve, Fred believed one must take risks and see possibilities in the unknown.

> *Be true to yourself but don't be afraid to take some risks. All boats are safe when moored in a harbor, but that's not what boats were built to do.*

> *If you're not living on the edge a little, you may be taking up too much of the space in the middle.*

As I read Fred's words, I could hear his voice, his gentle laughter in his office overlooking the skyline above the White House. I could see his sparkling eyes and that wise half smile when he knows he has you pegged.

Olivia was right. I may have been saying all the right things, but there was no doubt I'd been living for too long in the middle.

> *The girl wearily clings to the greasy pole. Her muscles ache, hands burn, fingers raw. Skin bloody from blisters, cuts, and bruises. Her breaking point near. Alone. Winds stir. The chill of thin mountain air sears her throat as she breathes. A storm looms on the horizon. The climb ever steeper, she wonders how long she can hold on. She dreams of rest and healing.*

Reluctant still, she summons her courage. Her voice scratchy and tired. She asks the universe if she has done enough, wondering how she will be judged. The storm comes. Winds scream. Rains whip like angry, heavy tears. Eyes closed, body shivering, the girl hangs on with all her might.

Then, calm. Light flickers. Warmth. The universe is holding her. "Yes, love, you have done enough."

Mom, are you ready? Olivia said, waking me up from my dream, her hand outstretched. Looking at my beautiful, kind, smart, strong, wise, very tall daughter, I saw a new girl warrior.

Taking hold of her hand, clear-eyed, and with a spot of courage, we stepped forward. It was then I felt my grip loosening as my fingers let go of the greasy pole.

For the first time in years, I felt free. With a tinge of nervousness, calm optimism, strength, weariness, and excitement, we looked ahead.

CHAPTER 10
Empowered

The gift of time and freedom is a beautiful thing.

It gave me the opportunity to see the world differently. With bigger, more abundant opportunities to fly higher and dream farther. Not small and confined to pathways, poles, or ladders that someone else assigned me.

I am no longer broken. I am no longer pretending. I am no longer silent.

With perspective, clarity, and strength, I get to do what I love most in both work and life: unravel mysteries, reimagine complex strategies to solve hard problems, and lend my voice to those who can't find their own. On my own terms. With freedom to speak out.

The most exquisite part of life today is that I'm no longer living a double life where I'm fighting for the rights of others while accepting less for myself and women like me. It makes me a better mom, a more authentic leader and honest role model.

I don't pretend to have "the answers" for how to solve women's equality challenges nor how to "fix" systems like Big Law. But I do know this.

I am stronger and more resilient than ever. Perhaps a little wiser.

I did many things exceedingly well. Yet, I see where I went wrong and what I might do differently now.

Many years ago, my mom told me it was important to work hard, prove my value, make my opportunities, and aim high. But she also said something else.

You are responsible for you, she'd say. *Your success is up to you.*

Looking back, I see now that I got caught up playing a game I was never supposed to win. The money and promises of greater opportunities were enticing. My desire to believe in the bet I made lured me into thinking I was more important to the system than I actually was.

As I played harder and accommodated more, I ceded power over my career to a system and leaders more than willing to take it—for far less than I was worth.

Until there was nothing left.

Yes, I did well. But it came at a price I could no longer pay.

Now that I've regained my power, one thing is certain. My power is no longer for sale.

THE ALLURE OF THE GAME

The allure of the game is harder to avoid than you think. It's even harder to see it when you are in it.

> *Why the hell did you stay so long?* A fellow warrior career mom asked after reading parts of this book. *Was it the money? Your love of the work? The need for recognition or satisfaction that you weren't beaten? This is nuts! It made me question my own choices!*

My friend was not alone. Many women face these same questions, including their own choices.

The answers always seemed to come back to two things: money and the allure of the game.

The Money.

The money was huge. We aren't independently wealthy. My salary paid for our house, our kids' college, retirement, the works.

To make matters worse, for years, I was hooked by the feeling I needed to make up lost ground. Yes, Big Law can ensnare anyone in its money trap.

What people fail to appreciate is that when women are systemically underpaid, the money trap feels more painful and personal. It feels like a lack of respect. It takes away some of your dignity. It makes you want to fight back. To prove you are worth more. To earn back what the system took.

Even when a woman can right the wrong or close the gap for the future, she'll still find herself trying to make up for lost time. The clock becomes a menacing monster, always ticking in the background. A reminder of time worked and lost, now and forever.

The money became even more complicated as I climbed higher. Money bought both freedom *and* captivity.

When women—many women—keep finding the courage to walk away, it should send a profound, resounding message to leaders that the system has serious problems.

The Game.

The cycle of the warped game was weirdly complex. Competitive by nature, I can see how I got caught up in an uneven game I believed I could win. Or, put another way, a game I refused to lose.

I kept telling myself if I could just hang on longer, I'd find a way to outsmart the system by being better, stronger, invincible.

I wanted to prove to myself and the world that I belonged and had more than earned my seat at the table. No matter what anyone said nor how I was treated. The more time passed, the harder it was to let go. Giving up, walking away, or surrendering felt like a bigger blow than the risks and trade-offs of the environment.

Yes, Big Law is no picnic. The system is competitive and hard for everyone. But for women seeking access, acceptance, equal treatment, and success in a male-dominated system, the reality is a harsh one.

For those who start and continue at a deficit, it's easy to become lulled into a false sense of security and hope. That feeling of importance, belief in partnership, and trust that we'll continue to rise if we just work harder, accommodate a little more, be the better team player, accept a little less for the greater good. . . . The cycle continues until it breaks.

For some reason, I couldn't accept that's how my story would end.

Yet, the true gift of my journey is coming out the other side. Realizing that in the haze of the battle, the dust of the foxhole, and the maze of the fight, I lost sight of a most important truth.

The one my kids held up in the mirror and made me see:

I have this one precious life to live.
I get to decide how to live it.
I get to decide my path forward.
I get to say I am worthy of infinitely more.

If the Big Law system isn't ready for women like me who want to be treated as equals, valued equitably, and appreciated for the many talents and gifts we bring to the table, then I have the power to choose. No one else.

Therein lies the truest gift of empowerment.

SILVER LININGS

What are other women supposed to do now, friends would ask. *Are you saying there is no hope for those left behind?*

No, hope is not lost. I don't think we should ever give up.

But clarity is a beautiful thing.

The truth is that system and behavior changes are hard. We need to be realistic about what's achievable in an imbalanced arena with forces that embrace the status quo.

Remember, women have been at this for decades. We can only do so much now or next year or in the next decade.

With realistic expectations, we can focus our power and energy on what we can control: the choices we make and the lines we draw in the sand.

If women leave jobs and leadership or the systems get a black eye, let leadership own it. Women should not take responsibility for fallout from decisions over which we have no control. We certainly shouldn't lie or participate in a ruse to shade the truth.

Further, we have the power of knowledge, our own choices, and strategic decision-making. We know that competing in the upper levels becomes exceedingly harder. Especially because women must continue to play on a tilted field with deficits embedded in the game.

The gift of empowerment is that we get to decide how long we want to play that game. If leadership makes little to no concessions or if the money isn't worth it, we can walk away.

But what do I do if I'm here now, you might ask. I know, if the younger version of *me* were reading this book, she would want concrete advice too. To *her* and my fellow women career warriors, I would say:

Like any career, the Big Law path can have benefits, costs, and risks. Be prepared to assess and reassess the trade-offs and pitfalls of the allure of the game.

Push for more transparency, candor, and realism wherever you can. Speak the truth about inequities. Press for change. But preserve your precious strength and power for what really matters. And stay alert so you can spot the mirage in the desert. The one that whispers, "keep going, work harder, you are almost there. . . ."

Think smarter and more strategically about your career. Own it. Maximize your potential to achieve your goals by learning the business while also being curious and open to opportunities and change. Adapt as needed. Remember, you don't need to burn bridges, but this isn't a family venture.

Business is business. As new opportunities arise, consider them seriously.

Most important, never forget to take care of yourself and pursue your life goals. You'll never get time back.

Other gems I would pass along?

1. Don't cede control of your career or give up your power to choose. Ever.

Too many of us fall into the trap of ceding power or control—and lose.

Avoiding the trap means undoing that chain around your ankles holding you to the desk or slave to the clock. Get up and look around, without guilt. Most of your male colleagues are doing it.

It is possible you'll have to change law firms to reset your salary someday. Or interview with other firms to understand your options. Or break free from the partner who promises you'll get that shared business revenue, but never delivers. Or leave to start your own venture.

Every year you stay or get stuck or feel trapped, these choices only get harder and feel more elusive. You must force yourself to constantly reassess.

One of the greatest gifts my first Big Law boss Bill gave to me was being candid about his retirement plans, and the fact that I'd have to stand on my own. No empty promises.

I wasn't thrilled but it forced me to get off my duff, learn the business, and own my Big Law career early.

Yet, I've seen that conversation go in another direction too many times. The false sense of security one gets from being a #2 can deliver uncomfortable surprises.

Money does strange things to people—even your beloved mentor, ally, sponsor, or champion. Big money translates to stature, acceptance, ego, and opportunity. People don't easily give that up. Some can't ever.

To make the big money, you must be a #1, the lead, a revenue generator.

Taking that leap is hard, scary, and lonely. If that's your goal, you'll want to be deliberate, strategic, and purposeful in your pursuit. Make sure you have thick skin and a solid suit of armor.

It's a tough, brutal climb but it can be done—at least for a while. Or you can launch in new directions. It's your choice. So long as you never forget to own your career—fully.

2. Set aside time from work to make yourself smarter, explore, and increase your power.

Get a coach. Write a business plan. Speak at outside conferences. Join business and executive networks. Non-lawyer networks. Yes, you must learn the craft of your chosen profession. But you also need to understand how businesses work—both inside and outside of your organization.

Inside, you want to understand how your organization makes money, the business structure, financial reports, the nitty gritty of the compensation system. Get to know the culture from different angles, the stories, the players. Understand where you fit in.

Businesses aren't always predictable or reliable. The more you know about the system, the better you'll understand your true opportunities for getting ahead and staying alive—or be able to show your business acumen when you want to leave.

Looking outside your organization is a smart career play. You'll find *extraordinary opportunities* outside the four walls that surround you. Even some that may present greater long-term security than the paycheck you now earn. It may not be what you want today but looking around helps you assess and reassess trade-offs. It also keeps your name in the game.

Oddly, knowing that you are fearless, known or sought after on the outside will shift perceptions of your value inside your own organization.

The more outside exposure you get, the greater your perceived flight risk, the greater your value, the better your ability to close the pay gap sooner.

There is only upside in exploring the outside world.

For those who fear change when a crossroad comes. Is leaving a risk? Yes. So is staying, waiting, and ceding control.

3. *"You may want to believe something different, but if someone tells you who they are, you should believe them."*

These are words of wisdom Gary Heil shared with me. Especially when I complained about interactions with Big Law leaders as I reflected on my career: whether responses were tone-deaf, radio silence, lack of progress, or not what I wanted to hear.

Leaders, by action and words, tell you who they are and how they feel about you. Pay attention to the signals.

I decided to compete on merit. Like many women though, I still took things to heart when there were contradictions about walking the talk, decisions that seemed unjust, or when gender issues played an unfair role. I confused fairness with business.

I say this with love, honor, and respect as a fellow warrior to the younger version of me:

> *Protect your power and energy. Give more energy to the things you can control. Keep your radar on and pay attention. Actions speak louder than words.*
>
> *Learn to recognize when you are being offered a one-sided deal. Beware of the trap, the allure of an unwinnable game, and getting stuck. Always keep handy the power to choose.*

While leaving may not be exactly what you want to do now, be as clear as you can with yourself for your reason to stay.

4. Beware of the lure of money.

One of my friends asked what I would say to those who can't "buy their freedom."

An interesting way to put it, I smiled. A younger version of me might think the same thing. For the record, I prefer to say I made an incredibly hard choice to break free of chains and a sweat factory to walk in the light and retake control of my life.

I made more money than some, not as much as others. I assure you I never made up the difference. Yet, year after year, no matter what I made, it was never "enough." It never made everything okay. You get trapped into thinking more is better. You seek approval, always worried about whether you are a favored child or sad disappointment.

Even today, leaving Big Law feels like a massive financial risk. Like most parents, we worry about that elusive question— how much is enough? Luckily, my family was persistent. My kids start leaving for college in four years. I won't get this time back, and I could no longer rationalize what I was giving up.

Staying longer wasn't going to change the system or make my life materially better. Nor would staying help any of my fellow warrior moms rise in the system or talk about inequities openly.

I am not saying everyone must or should leave. Nor that such an outcome is possible or even desirable for everyone.

So long as you reassess, understand, and own your choice. That alone is empowering.

IS THE SYSTEM FIXABLE?

This is a very hard question.

It wasn't lost on me that we were having *the same conversations we had twenty years ago*, and the number of women staying or leaving still hovers in only a marginally better range than over the last decade.

It felt like a broken record. The system churns on as all systems do.

A male friend and Big Law leader once asked me how he could help women in his firm. The conversation went something like this.

I want to help women succeed, he said. *What more can I do?*

What have you tried so far? I asked.

We've implemented flexible work schedules, sponsored women for speaking events and conferences, made sure there are leadership opportunities in the firm, encouraged and helped them to meet clients. . . .

The list went on.

As I listened, I noticed the steps helped with survival in the job and maybe provided incremental opportunities. They did not however address system inequities or changes that would translate to real power, higher salaries, or equality. They didn't even begin to touch the challenges I faced and that factored into my decision to leave.

> *For women to move up,* I explained, *they can't always be the #2. What are you doing to address that? Of the men in power positions, how many of them are willing to lose their trusted #2? How many are willing to assure she is viewed as competition for their paychecks—or perhaps even yours? And when she exceeds expectations, how many of them are willing to make good on promises?*

That started much a harder conversation. As we talked, I confirmed some men want to do the right thing and perhaps are trying. But they aren't willing to go the distance, even if they are great guys.

They don't always see the imbalances we feel. They think they're doing what they can. Still others feel they shouldn't be penalized for the old school attitudes that embedded inequities long ago, nor do they see the impact they still have on women peers.

Do I think we'll ever have true equality? No. But I think we can do much better.

With the benefit of distance, here's what I would offer to my friend and other Big Law leaders if they had an interest in a serious effort to retain women.

Treat the retention of women like your most important client challenge.

Do more to understand problems and their roots. Look at the system, culture, and people. Study, investigate, listen, invest. Understand the kind of environment that would make women want to stay.

Fix problems, even when fair and equitable changes mean someone else gets upset. If you are serious, you may have to make unpopular decisions or give up some unfair advantages. Some may have to, for once, take their turn to accept less based on merit or—like women have done for years—for the greater good to assure the business is stronger for the long game.

I ask you to resist the temptation to ask women for a list of improvements. That would just be another invisible load you'd be putting back on women to solve problems created by others. You'll have to be willing to roll up your own sleeves and do some of the hard work yourself.

What are some of the many benefits you've had the privilege of enjoying without thinking about it—maybe even a few things you've learned about from the experiences I've laid out in this book? Then, talk with your colleagues and peers, including women. Be open to hearing things you may not like or have appreciated.

Other things that could be considered:

Weed out anything that reeks of an inheritance model, the ole guys' network, avoiding hard compensation decisions, protecting those who undercut positive changes, and metrics that automatically penalize women.

Stop having women expect less and do more or sell programs that won't work. If retaining women isn't or can't be your priority, please say so. Then, we can make better decisions and have fewer regrets.

Stop getting certifications that don't match the real picture internally. It makes us lose faith in your intentions.

Become more human, empathetic, polite, and consistent. If people are working crazy hours, sacrificing time and personal lives, it's generally a good idea to show gratitude, appreciation, and concern for their well-being.

Lean in and listen when women raise issues or when they leave. Ask questions. Don't ignore them or their struggles. It may reflect other problems in the system. If you don't bother to ask, you can't say you don't know.

This is just a start.

Everyone wants an easy fix, like a playbook or checklist. Unfortunately, like all culture shifts, there are none. It's hard, gritty, uncomfortable work.

If you truly want to shift a culture or a system, brace up and dig in for the long haul. You'll need a lot of support.

The process involves identifying both visible and hidden challenges. The visible may seem easy to identify, but beware.

They're often impacted by invisible, hidden forces at the root of the problem: like attitudes, biases, greed, history, inheritance.

To the younger version of me, I say this:

> *For now, assume business systems like Big Law understand profit and the bottom line. Massive change won't happen unless the system resistance is met with an equal opposing competition that threatens revenue.*
>
> *It could take a generation to phase out sticky, arcane attitudes—assuming they haven't been converted to the dark side like the frog in the pot who can no longer see them.*
>
> *Until then, keep asking yourself: What trade-offs are you willing to make? How much are you willing to risk?*

Inevitably, there will only be hard realities and difficult choices. But always choices.

That is the truth.

EMPOWERMENT ON THE OTHER SIDE

While there is much to learn about our experiences inside Big Law or other entitlement systems, there is even more to explore outside.

A world where we have opportunities to consider strategies that might allow women to compete differently in the future.

Strategies that could put pressure on and eventually threaten coveted bottom lines of unbendable systems for future generations of sisters, daughters, and granddaughters.

We have no easy answers.

But solving hard problems is what women do well, right?

Imagine if we brought the village together to leverage our strengths to play a different game—and improve our odds of winning.

CHAPTER 11

Leveraging the Village

No drumbeats, I promised the girl.

It's just a conversation about finding ways to work together, perhaps some different options. It's not about rising up, or marching, or debating, or arguing . . .

We were still recovering from the drumbeats that overwhelmed us years ago.

When it's quiet, we can hear them.

DRUMBEATS

I was minding my own business, in the thick of heeding the *"work harder, keep your foot on the gas, buy help at home"* advice.

Then, out of left field, Sheryl Sandburg gave her famous Ted Talk about why we have too few women leaders, followed by her book *Lean In*. Sometime in between, Anne-Marie

Slaughter published her article *Why Women Still Can't Have It All* in *The Atlantic*, later followed by her book *Unfinished Business: Women Men Work Family*.

I remember amazing women sounding the alarm that new, great ideas were being born.

Then came the sounds of the drumbeats . . . like a ceremonial march to celebrate the next women's movement argument.

Women were tossing around ideas.

Women need to lean in more to opportunities, said Sheryl Sandberg.

Work harder. Keep your foot on the gas! said other women partners and executives.

Here's why women can't have it all, even if we work harder, said Anne-Marie Slaughter.

Women should think of the climb like a ladder, someone said.

No, a jungle gym, said another.

Wait, there's an elevator, the other woman said.

Hey ladies, we have a problem. Does anyone have a sledge-hammer? Nobody told us about the bulletproof, impenetrable glass ceiling, said yet another.

If I had a dollar for everyone who wanted to be me, said another senior woman partner.

There I was, a mom of young kids and an equity partner who was just barely managing her life.

I held my ears to drown out the sounds while hiding under my desk trying to do my work.

Stop! I told myself. *Don't listen to any of them!*

The mere topics of work-life balance or upward mobility seemed to cause great alarm, panic, self-doubt, arguments, cheers, and dissention in the ranks.

Yet, while we women argued, second-guessed, celebrated, and debated each other, the guys were drumming up business and cash. It was like they snuck by our conference rooms to play golf and cut a deal while we were distracted.

I was under my desk worrying whether I was enough, a decent mother, or . . . whether I was doing anything right.

Wait a second, I asked myself cynically one day, *Wouldn't it be Machiavellian if one of the guys paid off someone to start our argument?*

Seriously though. I didn't know what to make of it.

There were times when I thought women unintentionally and unwittingly made it harder for each other and easier for the guys. Of course, I've been there too.

Back then, discussions like these only made me question:

Whether I worked hard enough or not enough.

Whether I was a great warrior mom or a terrible mom.

Whether I was even worthy of being at a table among
elite women who seemed to be talking about whether
I leaned in enough or not.

Whether I was going about the climb in the right way
or even had the right color shoes.

I swore I would never do anything to start the drumbeats.

Last summer, when a women gave us the advice to work
harder, I heard the drumbeats in the distance.

I popped a couple of Tylenol to be safe. Thankfully, the beats
didn't last long.

Yet, I held my breath seeing our responses.

Women were appropriately unified in the view that we don't
need to work harder. But I was concerned about women
who went on to lay out all the herculean things we manage
in a single day. Even I had to admit some descriptions were
quite impressive.

At one time I might have celebrated these women, even
envied them, and upped my game.

Now, I wanted to warn my younger warrior sisters about Burnout. Let them know what she feels like when she's really angry.

Send them hugs. Praise them. Then tell them that it's okay to rest.

To my fellow warrior career moms, I would like to invite you to *not do it all.*

The system doesn't make our sacrifices worth it.

Before you know it, your kids will be going off to college while you pay for their tuition—and the tuitions of the kids of that guy down the hall who took credit for your work. Enjoy your kids instead. Regrets like that would stink.

With masses of women reconsidering careers and the people worried about it, I suggest we encourage our industries and leaders to accept "our invitation" to get off their butts and start doing their part.

Meanwhile, let's reassess our trade-offs, do less accommodating and heavy lifting. Equalize the workload a bit wherever we can. Slow down. Stop doing more. Breathe a little.

Then, let's think creatively and strategically about where to go from here. Perhaps a little differently than we've done before.

CONFESSIONS, MINDSET SHIFTS, AND VILLAGES

I do *not* have all the answers, but I do know one thing: I've needed a mindset shift for some time.

Sitting here now, I'm still in shock that I've written a book that focuses on gender issues—of all things. Given the warrior, tough girl theme, that might seem a little surprising to you too. A contradiction.

The truth is I've always been uncomfortable taking on gender fights or causes.

I'd fight for individuals, and mentor or sponsor fellow women behind the scenes. But I didn't do causes. It wasn't just because I was tired and worn down by the end of the day. It seemed inconsistent with the approach I'd adopted of competing on merit and owning the room as the warrior I'd become.

Yet, there was more.

As best I can unravel now, three big issues:

> First, I thought the fabric of our women villages was frayed. We seemed to have too much judgment and criticism of the impossible choices each of us face— and not enough love, embracing of those choices, and unwavering support.

Second, I'd been in enough women's group meetings over the years. I didn't think we were getting very far. We accomplished things when we got legitimately pissed off, like the #MeToo movement where brave women called out illegal, outrageous behavior. But, in other areas, our progress felt stalled. Women's lunches and conferences weren't spurring business opportunities. They felt more social. Some felt like bitch sessions. The village didn't seem to be moving forward.

Third, I didn't like the way we competed—with each other. Professionally or personally. While a woman might find some to support her, she faced an equal number who were ready to take her out with a sharp elbow or bat to the kneecap. And an equal number of spectators who would do nothing to help. The dynamic made me want to protect myself, even when standing with my sisters.

I was one of those women who left the village.

At times, I didn't have the protective gear I needed to shield myself from judgments I feared or worried about, or that made me second-guess myself. Truthfully, I already had that second-guessing thing covered pretty well—as my own worst critic. I didn't need more voices chiming in.

So, I maintained a close circle of women friends but, otherwise, made excuses and shied away.

I know we all have those stories where we've made assumptions about another woman who worked, didn't work, or worked part-time.

I also know the knee-jerk reaction to criticize, chat about, or even bash someone who is perceived as not doing enough, or who raises the prickly topic of playground arguments, or who may seem like she doesn't quite fit in.

The truth is we are all doing our best to navigate our way through this complicated life. I've always wished we would do more to embrace and honor that. Assume the best in each other, lend a hand, and never assume anyone has it all figured out.

Here's an example of how this played out in the job. It's the kind of thing that made being a senior woman in a male-dominated world an even lonelier place to roam.

I need to say I'm sorry, said my partner unexpectedly when I shared that I was leaving the firm.

I feel bad we never joined forces, she continued, as I held my breath waiting to see where this was going.

I wasn't very nice to you, she said. *I felt like the men pitted us against each other. I regret that now.*

I didn't know what to say.

My partner wasn't kidding when she owned up that she wasn't particularly nice. In fact, that was probably an understatement. I learned early on the hard way that, if I wanted to avoid a knife fight, I'd have to work in a parallel universe where our paths crossed as little as possible. It wasn't worth the aggravation or the battle. It would only assure deeper wounds.

Yet now that I was no longer a threat, I had to listen to her bemoan lost opportunities and share in her guilt that she took "the bait." Whatever that was.

I appreciated her gesture (sort of), but I didn't really buy the bait story.

Even if it was true, I thought, *we can't blame the men when we fall for it. Taking the bait isn't a luxury we as a sisterhood have.*

Why do women do this to each other? I asked a friend later. *We are the worst when it comes to competition. We get in each other's way and let someone else, usually a guy, walk right by us.*

I don't know. It's maddening and happens everywhere, my friend shared. *You should write about that.*

Too often, our mindset is to compete for "available" seats or opportunities instead of creating more.

I've never liked how those competitions play out. I tried to avoid them. Women end up looking bad. The guys seem to enjoy it. If the guys are crafty, they'll take advantage of it.

What's the woman head-to-head competition thing about anyway? a friend asked.

And why do some, once they get to a table, play both sides and cut deals that alienate them from their sisters just to stay there? another friend brought up.

There were no good answers to those questions. But here was a better question.

Why not turn our attention to fight the real fight that needs to be fought?

If we can compete on merit and honor each other—because we are smart, capable, and big-hearted—let's support each other in doing that and be more tactical in our approach.

If we go for the one seat someone else tells us is available and check a box for diversity, we lose.

If we work together, take the seat, and also compete for the seat some guy is sitting in, that takes the fight to a whole new level. After all, it's likely we're paying for the seat anyway, right? Why not get that one too?

One woman director told me that one boardroom seat is a token, two is competition, and three is a quorum where we can finally get something done. So why not go for three?

I'm not saying it would be easy or men aren't qualified or that we should be "given" their jobs or their seats on a silver platter.

But I am saying that there are many highly qualified, hard-working women who get shit done and shouldn't have to work ten times as hard for the privilege of "earning" a seat that was reserved for a guy.

I'm also saying to women that if we spent less time elbowing each other over a rickety chair a pack of guys say we can have, imagine what progress we could make in achieving more?

When it comes to our peer women and allies, I hope we re-think our strategy.

There's ugly competition. There's worthy competition. I can fight in the former but, given the option, I'll pick the latter. It's even more fun if I can fight alongside my sisters.

Then, *we can decide* how many of us get seats at tables, a place in the room, or a role in the game. In fact, if we did it right, we could own that table.

This is what the idea is all about.

AN IDEA: LEVERAGING OUR DIVERSE TALENTS AND CHOICES AS ASSETS

What if we start exploring how to embrace, leverage, and use our diverse talents and choices as assets? Not as points of contention, comparison, judgment, or topics for debate.

What if we used our individual, fabulous, courageous, brilliant choices to play the game smarter?

After all, one of the beautiful things about our gender is the diversity, uniqueness, and range of gifts among us.

Is it possible to start seeing a world beyond brick walls, doors, ceilings, poles, or ladders?

Imagine if even our visuals became more limitless?

If we thought of our journeys in a way that allowed us to adapt to inevitable highs, lows, winds, currents, and twists in our beautiful, messy lives?

Not along a rung that doesn't fit our shoe size or style or offer support we may need in the moment. Nor taking the risk of waiting in a limited world, but of embracing the possibility of flying beyond it.

This was the visual I asked my son, Jack, to create, now the sketch that appears in the epigraph of this book. It's the visual I asked my daughter, Olivia, to imagine and hold close to her heart for her own future. Both Olivia and Jack decided on the infinity symbol to represent opportunities for women of the future. Jack added the magic touch of his treasured birds that embodied words of wisdom we heard from one of my favorite leadership teachers, Dr. Bertrand Piccard:

> We must change altitude to find other levels, other influences, strategies, solutions, or answers that will automatically push us in another direction. We must be ready at every moment to modify our vision of the world if we want to

steer our destiny around the obstacles and invent our own
future instead of being a victim of it.

WHAT IF?

What if, in Big Law, for example, women of the future built or started to expand powerhouse boutique law firms or created law firm alliances that competed in ways that not only showed true depth of diversity of thought and talent, but that also embodied the values and business principles we want to see more of? Like price points and other metrics that made sense and worked for all our varied goals and needs.

If that alternative was available, especially one that offered the right brain power and solutions, without doubt it would get some attention. Not just among idealistic law students and the future of law, 50 percent of whom are women. Clients would pay attention. And it might be the kind of bottom-line revenue competition pressure that someday gets the attention of Big Law. It's hard to imagine that the business model of infinitely higher hourly rates in a finite day will be a lasting long-term play.

Envision how conversations might shift if losing enough of us and the brain power we bring to problem solving ran an even bigger risk of losing an actual piece of their pie, as opposed to a blemish they need to cover-up in their diversity track record.

You may be thinking, O*kay Amy, nice try, but what is actionable now?*

My response to that is, *I understand the frustration but ask you this: Is actionable what we've been doing? Are we willing to continue to throw our positive energy and sweat equity down the drain in a system that has told us what it is? Or do we want to dream a little and take a run at something else?*

Imagine what we could accomplish if we spent more time on ideas that could matter or that weren't putting our future in the hands of people and systems that resist change. Now that we've been having the same conversations for twenty (or thirty or more) years, I'm suggesting perhaps we shift at least some of our precious energy and focus to something new or different or bigger. If not the law firm idea, perhaps come up with something else.

The only way Big Law and other industries will start to see women differently is not: if we march or yell (they'll just hunker down and wait for us to stop), or if we complain, quit, or sue (they'll pay for the settlement, implement a couple new policies, and paint the walls a different color).

I am not saying marching, yelling, complaining, quitting, or suing have no value. I'm just saying that it's sort of become a never-ending negative cycle we don't seem to win.

From where I sit today, the only way I see material change is if male-dominated industries start seeing women as competition in a different way.

And then,

I wonder why we should bother wasting our energy trying to change these systems or those who run them.

Wouldn't it be faster to create that world for ourselves? Why not reap the benefits faster?

It's still a long-term play, no doubt.

> For those of us who are older in the industry today where some of these actions may take more time, it could be our contribution is the value of our experience, mentoring, championing, sponsoring, investing, and educating.

> For those of us who are younger in the industry today and thinking of pivoting, it could be the opportunity is to team up and explore new venture opportunities.

> For those of us who are still in school or thinking about graduate school, it could be considering a healthy complement of business and entrepreneurship courses to maximize options later.

These "what if" ideas aren't necessarily new. In fact, as I look at the world with a new perspective, they are already happening in different ways.

Perhaps I was too busy to see them.

Or perhaps the opportunity was never as clear in my mind as it is now.

WHAT DO YOU DO WITH AN IDEA?

On my leadership journey, the one I dragged my family along to experience over this last year, we learned that women are already pursuing lofty goals and paying it forward in their own amazing ways that could be game changers, especially if we take the time to learn from them.

I'd like to live in a world where we take the opportunity to think bigger and wider, not narrow and crushing.

In the year the world went mad, I went on the hunt for books to inspire my kids. We looked at them again when they faced decisions on school changes, evolutions with friend groups, or building the courage to try something new.

In my costume as the cool, wise mom, I came across a series of kid books by Kobi Yamada, illustrated by Mae Besom. One was called *What Do You Do with an Idea?* It sits on the shelf in my office.

The book begins with the story of a young child who had a curious experience. . .

> *One day, I had an idea. "Where did it come from? Why is it here?" I wondered, "What do you do with an idea?" (Yamada, 2013).*

The idea is a small, mystical egg-like creature that wears a crown and follows the boy around. At first it seems strange and fragile. The boy pretends it doesn't belong to him. But it continues to follow him.

Worried about what people might say, the boy tries to hide *the idea*. Yet, *the idea* stays with him. He admits to himself that there's something sort of magical and special about it. He's secretly happier when it's around. As time passes, *the idea* needs food and attention. As it grows bigger, they become friends. Yet, when people make fun of it, he questions himself and almost gives up.

But the boy can't walk away. He likes *the idea* even more. He decides to protect it, work with it, create a safe space to dream with it. *The idea* makes him feel alive and shares its secrets that help the boy see things differently.

Then, one day, *the idea* changes, spreads its wings, takes flight, and bursts into the sky.

I don't know how to describe it, but it went from being here to being everywhere. It wasn't just a part of me anymore. . .

Now it was part of everything.

And then, I realized what do you do with an idea.

You change the world.

* * *

So, before I go,

I'd like to introduce you to some incredible people who started out with an idea, a chance, and a choice.

Who didn't allow themselves to be stuck or pigeon-holed. Who weren't deterred by what people would say or might think.

Who launched their ideas. And who, without a doubt, are in fact changing the world.

It's just a taste of the kinds of possibilities that exist.

And a window into what we can accomplish . . .

If we try.

CHAPTER 12

Game Changers

What if . . . ?

I love this kind of question more than any other. It comes from a place of curiosity and openness. A place where possibilities still exist. A place where people can be creative. Even dream a little.

Imagine if we all did a little more creating and dreaming— and less fighting.

Meeting people who are dreamers and doers gave me hope that there are other realities worth pursuing, other ways of thinking, and more to life than what I'd settled for in a climb on a pole.

People out there are changing the world in important ways.

It wasn't because someone gave them a roadmap. It wasn't because someone gave them directions. It wasn't because someone made their lives easy.

It was because they took the road less traveled. They took some chances. And dared to dream in ways that were big or small or brave.

The stories told here are among those that motivated me to punch through that brick wall.

To see what was on the other side. To recharge my energy. To rebuild my courage.

To explore a little. Dream a little. Create a little. Rest a little. Live a little.

To let my mind wander.

And wonder *what if. . .?*

CREATING ALLIANCES, BUSINESS OPPORTUNITIES, ELEVATING AND SUSTAINING WOMEN LEADERS

After years of being worn down by the climb, I wasn't really open to new ideas on networking until I saw a private, for-profit organization named Chief and its catchy LinkedIn profile mantra that captured my attention:

> *We're not waiting for a seat at the* table—*we're building* our own. (Chief, LinkedIn, 2021).

Founded by Carolyn Childers and Lindsay Kaplan and funded by venture capitalists and members committed to the advancement of women, Chief connects women leaders across industries to drive more women into positions of power and, more importantly, keep us there.

All too often, women are promoted into leadership roles with little or no support. With precious little peer understanding of what women must juggle to operate at peak performance over sustained periods of time—and too few of us in these positions to have ready-made support groups in our organizations—Chief offers a critical alternative.

The need to avoid losing women to burnout or failures that could have been avoided with better preparation is very real. Chief aims to fill that gap by investing in women, education, and awareness, and helping women build their own peer board of directors, advisors, and allies.

It's not fluff. I became one of them. Chief offers senior women the ability to seek advice and input from other senior women across organizations in an array of power positions ranging from founders and owners to C-suite executives to directors and leaders. The level and sophistication of the dialogue offers not only ongoing support among women in the upper tiers of organizations but is also proof that women are thinking about their futures differently, more intentionally and strategically.

The commonality that the community shares is changing the face of leadership, it is being a woman in business, and what it means to carry that weight and to wrestle with all of the changes that have come over the last decade of working in

America, said Lindsay Kaplan in a recent interview for *Jewish Insider.*

Which is why I'm thrilled to be part of Chief and finding ways to give back through the exceptional network they offer. I am finding that as much as I give, I get back in spades from this incredibly talented group of powerhouse women.

What if, as we make our climbs, we finally had the same kind of mastermind groups and personal boards of directors that men have had forever?

What if, as we arrived at the table, we explored strategies and tactics with our Chief sisters to assure we found ways to open the doors for others, so that we weren't so alone?

What if we used our own powerful networks to get more women in positions of leadership and power so our daughters and granddaughters saw a different composition of faces at the top when they arrive?

NO BARRIERS

What do you mean your organization has no barriers? How is that possible? I asked Amanda Doyle, trying to understand how others figured out ways of achieving success differently.

A former Big Law lawyer and business manager for her sister Glennon Doyle, Amanda is also a leader in nonprofit Together Rising. Amanda explained the intention behind Together Rising was to create an organization *without barriers.* No stranger to the unending limitations of bureaucracy, Amanda shared:

> *We saw the power of Glennon's very large community of followers when there was a call to action or a cry for help. She was able to raise an incredible amount of money through the small donations and generosity of her followers. Creating an organization with no barriers was consistent with our thinking and mission: To achieve beyond what people think is possible. That mindset makes us more flexible and open to ideas to solve hard problems, and we do.*

Together Rising isn't like a sisterhood; it is one. Amanda describes it as a "super charged, warm space." Its mission is to turn collective heartbreak into effective action using what they refer to as time-limited "love flash mobs" to raise crowdsourced funds online.

With a maximum donation of twenty-five dollars and the ability to mobilize communities of friends and strangers quickly, Together Rising's capacity for giving back to communities is truly remarkable. As an example, in just one 2018 campaign with a call to action, Glennon raised $1 million in just nine hours during an emergency Love Flash Mob to provide advocates and legal representation for children separated from their families at the border. Unlike other nonprofits, 100 percent of the money received by Together Rising goes to the cause.

Liz Book, another passionate leader, described one of Together Rising's strengths as its ability to harness the power to find caring people sitting behind their computer screens wondering how they can help. It was how they found me one summer day in the middle of the COVID pandemic, through the power of an email, a connection, and a wish to be of service.

To hear them talk about their belief in the mission, their sisters, and the power of people to work together even in small ways to do hard things makes it impossible not to wonder what else is achievable.

Which is why a portion of the proceeds of this book will be donated to Together Rising's mission.

What if we organized our own brains and other business models around the mindset of "no barriers"?

What if we explored the idea of more sisterhoods where the only topic of discussion was how to get it done—not whether we were capable?

What if we graciously acknowledged and embraced each other's impossible choices and affirmed through our words and actions our unwavering support for each other?

DREAMERS AND DOERS

One of my other favorite connections was Melissa Kilby, the Executive Director and courageous leader of Girl Up, a global leadership development initiative of the United Nations Foundation.

Melissa is a dreamer and a doer on just about *every* level. She's found ways to use the winds of change to expand networks of girls and women around the world who are—without any doubt—changing their path for the future.

Girl Up has a wide range of initiatives to train, encourage, and inspire girls and young women to embrace the power they hold as leaders, entrepreneurs, and citizens so they can be a force for gender equality and social change. Melissa shared that, to date, Girl Up's leadership development programs have impacted 95,000 girls through 5,000 clubs in nearly 130 countries and all fifty US states—and counting.

When Olivia and I spoke with Melissa in the summer of 2020, she had just wrapped up the first-ever virtual Girl Up annual conference. In a year when most nonprofits struggled, this conference was a smashing success that proved what can happen when one has the courage to see opportunity in disruption.

As the world was shutting down in 2020, Melissa and her team decided it would be the wrong time to cancel an opportunity for girls to connect, especially when they might need it most. Girl Up pivoted the conference to become a first-ever online event. It drew big-name speakers like Michelle Obama, Hillary Clinton, and Priyanka Chopra and resoundingly impressed important corporate donors. Offering inspiration and encouragement to be a force for each other no matter where they lived, the attendee list grew from hundreds to thousands of girls representing every Girl Up club in the world.

A humble steward of the Girl Up team, change maker, and innovative thinker, Melissa empowers those around her to live up to their infinite potential.

> *The idea is to help girls everywhere understand there are no bounds or limits to defining what a girl is or who she could be. We are creating a new generation of changemakers,* Melissa shared with me and Olivia.

> *No matter what hand life has taught you, we must pay it forward. Girls have great power when we stand together.*

Which is why a portion of the proceeds of this book will be donated to support Girl Up's mission.

What if career women learned a few lessons from girls who believe there are no bounds or limits to defining who we are?

What if we found infinitely more ways to stand with our daughters and the next generation of women leaders to help them see wider paths with fewer sacrifices and more choices?

What if we became less afraid of change?

INVESTING IN THE NEXT GENERATION OF LEADERS TO BUILD A STRONGER FUTURE

Carla Cuglietta is an inspiring former teacher who found her passion in developing youth leaders. Now, a humanitarian and co-founder of global nonprofit YoungLeaders. World, Carla and her husband Tyler Waye are inspiring a new generation of leaders to pursue purpose and a vision that comes from within. And they encourage young people to contribute to their communities to make the world a better place. They not only believe in unlimited possibilities, they help others believe in them too.

Carla said once to Olivia and me, *leadership and citizenship are about setting a new direction and inviting others to come with you to create a better tomorrow for those around them.*

That is exactly how Carla lives her own life. She walks the walk and the talk. The lessons Carla shared formed the basis of Olivia's arguments to me—about living a more authentic life, walking my talk, leading from my own internal compass, and doing more to help others in need.

You can either lead life, or life will lead you. So, you lead. We're focused on helping young people find a purpose and vision that comes from within, not goals influenced by parents, friends, or social trends. To create a generation of young people leading for personal growth and collective good.
—Carla Cuglietta, humanitarian, leader, visionary, co-founder of YoungLeaders.World

Which is why a portion of the proceeds of this book will be donated to support the mission of YoungLeaders.World.

What if we all took time to share our lessons learned with young leaders of tomorrow?

What if we took time to talk with a young stranger who needed inspiration on some random fall day and helped change her perspective on how she saw the world?

What if we all took the time to create more villages to help those less fortunate, and used those opportunities to inspire ripples of gratitude to those who give and receive?

MANY HANDS MAKE LIGHT WORK

This is the motto of the board of directors of the Women's Bar Association Foundation in Washington, DC. It's a smart, diversely talented, creative, and persistent team of women focused not on profile or well-funded, big money foundations and corporate sponsors, but on grants that fund local organizations providing legal aid and related services to underserved women and girls in our local community of Washington, DC.

The foundation supports dreams that are massively important to women. For example, it sponsors and aids organizations that help women and girls break free from abusive relationships, support caretakers and the elderly, advocate for access to job-related justice, and fight for fair-housing rights and access to critical support services in our communities and courts.

When you give to the Foundation, you are helping women and girls successfully access the legal system—improving their employment and housing situations, reducing their stress, and allowing them to get on with their lives, helping to lift them and their families out of poverty and traumatic situations, said Rachel Hardwick, president of the WBA Foundation.

Which is why a portion of the proceeds of this book will be donated to support the Women's Bar Association Foundation mission.

What if we applied the approach of leveraging our varied skills to achieve important objectives in our many communities, and appreciated the many gifts different women can bring to any table?

What if we found more opportunities to support those in our communities who, with a chance, an opportunity, or support, might become another woman leader who would pay it forward for others?

What if we all took the time to see more of the world around us because we are more than just timekeepers or climbers or stewards of programs never intended to succeed—because we believe each of us is worth infinitely more?

WORDS OF WISDOM ON THE PATH FORWARD

I know I'm not alone in saying that equality has a long way to go. I also know that there are many women out there who believe we can leverage our skills and ideas to do it better. There are also women who have forged ahead.

SEEING BEYOND BARRIERS AND CHAMPIONING AN IDEA

Mindy Scheier's son, Oliver, was born with a rare form of muscular dystrophy. After seeing him struggle dressing himself and worrying about him, Mindy leveraged her experience in the fashion industry. With a lot of grit, she developed adaptive clothing lines for people with disabilities (PWD), blowing open a previously untapped market of buying power and shining light on the will of PWDs to be seen as equals. As founder of nonprofit Runway of Dreams and CEO of a for-profit talent agency for PWDs, Mindy says that while spearheading Gamut Management wasn't the life she envisioned, she now couldn't see it any other way. She is courageous, positive, and relentless in her support of the PWD community. She's proven where there's a will, there's a way.

Just because something has been done one way does not mean it can't be done another way.
—MINDY SCHEIER, FOUNDER, CEO, CHANGEMAKER, MOM

PIVOTING, TRUSTING YOURSELF, AND EMBRACING CHANGE

Lauren Liess is an interior designer, author, and mom of five kids. In 2020, she designed the Southern Living 2020 Idea House in Asheville, North Carolina. Lauren leveraged her passion by turning her fixer-upper home into her own portfolio of natural, livable designs, blogging about the transformations in real time. Then, she sold it, flipped the next house, and then the next. Letting people live her transformations launched her brand as a wildly successful designer. She attributes her success to being grounded yet nimble and adaptive. And she's learned to trust herself and follow her instincts.

When we trust our gut, it always works out, she says. Change is an opportunity to bet on yourself. Shaking off the shackles is when we find freedom and are the happiest.

—LAUREN LIESS, INTERIOR DESIGNER, AUTHOR, ENTREPRENEUR, STAR OF THE HGTV PILOT "BEST HOUSE ON THE BLOCK," MOM

TURNING UNCERTAINTY INTO A COMPETITIVE EDGE

Alexa von Tobel is among the early investors in Chief. During the financial crisis in 2008, she left Harvard business school and founded a company called LearnVest, whose business objective was focused on giving everyday Americans financial advice, especially women. After seeing her mother struggle when her father died, Alexa never wanted anyone to experience that again. Her platform not only gave users a full picture of their finances, but offered explanations and options in plain English so that busy people could make intelligent decisions about investing. In 2015, just days before she had her first child, Alexa sold LearnVest for $375 million. Today, she's an author and CEO of her own venture capital firm, Inspired Capital. She's helping women launch innovative new companies and investing in organizations that support women leaders of today and the future. In a recent interview, she shared some wisdom on turning uncertainty into an asset.

None of us knows how long this hybrid world will last. But you can use this environment as a competitive edge: It's never been easier to meet investors and build relationships across the country.
—ALEXA VON TOBEL, VENTURE CAPITALIST,
SERIAL ENTREPRENEUR, AUTHOR, MOM

HONORING TIME

Amy Knapp's daughter faced challenges after contracting meningitis as an infant. Amy's wildly successful calendar business had its origins in her efforts to keep track of Natalie's needs, doctors, and the dreaded family schedule. She's inspired millions of others to both manage *and honor* their time in the process, including my daughter, Olivia.

Humility is a trait I desire most. Yes, I've faced challenges in my life that created new challenges managing my time. I've learned that if you treat it as just a calendar that is what it will be. If you respect it as something where people are inviting you into their lives and personal spaces, it will become something different.
—AMY KNAPP, FOUNDER, ENTREPRENEUR, AND MOM

CITIZENSHIP

Sue Boardman, in her second career, became the architect of the Gettysburg Foundation Executive Leadership Program called "In the Footsteps of Leaders." Our family spent a day with Sue and her team on the battlefields, hearing stories about battlefield history and politics, strategies and tactics, tragedy and triumphs, rhetoric and facts. Yet, her most important advice to our kids was this:

Be careful of rhetoric, influencers, disruptors. Remember that each person has his or her own perspectives, motives, and history. Do your own homework. Decide what you believe. Be open to new ideas. No matter what you do, lead yourself and do it with your heart not just your head. Be the one who adapts to create greater understanding, awareness, and citizenship. Above all, never forget that you have endless gifts and be confident that you will always be able to pivot.

—SUE BOARDMAN, AUTHOR, HISTORIAN,
VISIONARY, AND ARCHITECT OF THE GETTYSBURG
FOUNDATION EXECUTIVE LEADERSHIP PROGRAM

IS CHANGE REALLY POSSIBLE?

In one of our debates, I remember vigorously arguing with Gary that change was possible if people wanted it badly enough. He pointed out how culture and human nature naturally resists new directions. It's not that it is impossible, but it isn't easy either.

All fair points, I had to concede. But, what if? I wondered.

So, you're one of those dreamers who wants to change the world? Gary smiled.

After pausing to think and digging past the healthy brick layers of cynicism and pessimism I've built up over the years, I found a little light shining through the mortar.

Yes. I guess I am, I said, grinning back at Gary, without really knowing why but feeling strangely stronger for recognizing a glimmer of hope.

It's not just that the alternative is too depressing.

But because it's what I hope to pass on to my kids.

Besides, in the end, isn't every one of us worthy of infinitely more?

Another world is not only possible,
she is on her way. On a quiet day,
I can hear her breathing.

—ARUNDHATI ROY

Epilogue: Freedom

What is life like today? And what does the future hold?

It's an interesting question. The past year has been a whirl-wind of change. Seeing light and feeling freedom brings me a strange, yet beautiful, empowered sense of peace. Not to mention a strong belief that I have much more to give to the world, and that my career has a few more lives to live.

I have no doubt that advocacy will be in my future in differ-ent forms—both in my work and through renewed advocacy to help create more awareness, wider pathways, and unlim-ited possibilities for women and girls in the future. (My son, Jack, reminds me not to leave him out. After all, he says, he wants to be part of the solution so that his success is fairly earned alongside his many friends, both girls and boys. Fair point.)

I honestly do not know what the future holds.

For the first time in as long as I can remember, I am actually okay with that. I am letting the future unfold gracefully and allowing the universe to guide me a bit.

I am learning to navigate a world devoid of über command centers—a world without chains, hamster wheels, greasy poles, and clocks ticking. It feels so powerful and empowering to treasure time instead of fearing or resenting it.

I am just beginning to understand what "freedom" truly means.

What does it feel like you ask?

Let me tell you a story about an afternoon during our family's incredible, crazy leadership journey.

It was one of my favorite days when Olivia taught me what it felt like to be free. I didn't fully appreciate it at the time, but it's an afternoon I know now that I'll carry with me forever.

It was the Saturday after Justice Ruth Bader Ginsburg died. A melancholy day when Olivia and I had a date with another legend named Diane Crump, fifty years after she was the first woman jockey to race in the Kentucky Derby at Churchill Downs.

We "prepared" for the interview, of course. I wanted to be respectful of Diane's time.

Diane lives in a modest house on a tree-lined street in the country. She is small in stature, shy, reserved. She gives off an almost steely vibe.

At the start, Diane was polite and a bit distant. I didn't think we'd stay very long. Yet, for whatever reason, the afternoon unfolded unexpectedly. Diane and Olivia started to hit it off, bonding over Diane's beloved service dogs, Olivia's love of horses, and a conversation about faith.

As I watched and listened to my daughter, I saw this other side of her. Softer, genuine, true blue, relaxed, warm, funny. A deeper thinker. Diane warmed up too. We spent hours with Diane that day, hearing her stories, about the launch of her new book, and her memories of her mom. When it came time to leave in the early evening, it was harder than we thought—like we were leaving an old friend.

Mom, you have no idea what it's like talking with someone like Diane. Someone who knows what it's like to feel free, said Olivia as we were driving east from Warren County, Virginia, toward home on a beautiful, hot summer evening.

How would you know what it's like to be free? Tell me about that, I said.

Well, it's hard to explain, but it's why I love going to Betsy's farm. It's in the middle of nowhere, surrounded by fields and horses and grasses and dragonflies. It quiet, peaceful. No one expects me to be anyone other than me, she continued.

Imagine you close your eyes. You hop on a horse bareback, you just ride. Through the tall grasses, in the sun, with not a care in the world. It's like all the weight falls off my shoulders. My armor. The expectations. The judgments. The pressure. They all fall away.

That's what freedom feels like, Mom.

As I looked over at Olivia, her eyes were closed, the sunroof was open, the light was fading in the sky. Stray hair from her messy bun blew softly on her face. She was smiling.

In that moment, I remember Diane's parting advice to Olivia.

My whole life, I've done what I loved. I hope you do the same. Don't let anyone talk you out of your dreams. And remember, never let anyone tell you that you can't do something or that you aren't good enough. You are.

Isn't that the kind of advice we should all ascribe to?

No matter our age.

To you my fellow warrior women, warrior career moms, and warriors of the future.

As we weigh the trades we are willing to make, the bargains we are willing to strike, the uneven battles we are asked to fight, our worth and our value, our choices and pathways ahead, I leave you with this.

May you always believe in yourself, the unlimited possibilities this world has to offer, and your power to choose.

May you find strength, courage, and empowerment while remaining true to who you are. Take care of yourself, protect your time, embrace your gifts, stay curious, hold onto your purpose.

May you always keep that sense of wonder and forever have faith that you can do anything you set your mind to.

And finally, no matter what pathway you choose, may you always fly free.

Acknowledgments

There is no doubt it takes a village to walk through this crazy life of high wire juggling acts, impossible mom feats, career climbing, and motherhood. Perhaps an even bigger village than I'd ever realized. To say I have been humbled by the experience of reflection across a range of experiences is an understatement.

To Regina Stribling, my friend and editor, I start with you. Without you, there would be no book. Over a year ago, you told me what this book would be about. You graciously showed up each week, grinned at my storytelling and gently reminded me—again and again. But I said *absolutely not*. Yet, when I returned only a few months ago in 2021, having been followed by an egg with a crown for many months, you graciously and humbly took me under your wing and shared the magic of your gifts of writing and storytelling. A heroine's journey, you said. Using words to paint pictures, to elicit emotions, to make a point in a non-lawyerly way. To share an experience that would resonate with many more women who are just like me. You joined me in laughter, tears, frustration, sadness, and hope. You made me a better writer, a better person, and helped me choose freedom by sharing my story. You are the best editor and guide a girl could ask for—a wizard with words, a calming force, a wise soul. I am forever in your debt.

Eternal gratitude and love to my family.

This book and my journey today would not be a reality without the love, patience, humor, courage, creativity, endurance, compassion, tolerance, wisdom, and open-mindedness of my family. What started as my fancy effort to teach them a few things about leadership turned into a bigger opportunity for them to show me what is most important in life. And how leading myself and choosing freedom could reveal greater possibilities for pursuing my passions and life purpose.

To my daughter, Olivia, and my son, Jack, thank you for your bravery and love. For your willingness to learn, explore, take courses, watch videos, share in interviews, edit drafts, and talk about ideas. For making me laugh, for sharing your creative talents. For listening and *hearing* important lessons that I wasn't willing to hear myself and, in turn, offering your wisdom to help me see my worth, my purpose—and some holes in that brick wall that offered new pathways. For believing in me and then reminding me to believe in myself.

To my husband, Sid, for your love, encouragement, and patience through this book journey, career, and life shift. From our late night/early morning brainstorming and editing sessions to you pivoting to cover kid and house stuff while I recovered from surgery or feverishly wrote and rewrote, I'm truly grateful not only for your love, unlimited support, encouragement, and load sharing, but also for your willingness to "dig in," be open to hard conversations and to understand tough gender issues. For being not just a husband and partner in life, but becoming a true ally. I am so excited to see where life takes us from here, whether it be watching the fast-paced action of our kids and their teams on the volleyball court or lazy afternoons by the fire—even in August when it makes your bride happy. Thank you for honoring and believing in me.

To my warrior mom, Kathleen, you gave me the guts and the strength to shoot for the moon and aim high. I would not have made it this far without the kind of grit, resourcefulness, and determination you instilled in me as a kid and into adulthood. I am so proud of your accomplishments, especially now that I have a window into what it was like for women in generations before. Thank you for blazing pathways. To my dad, Dennie, for teaching us to work hard, to never give up, and not to take any grief from any of the guys. To my siblings, Moira, Megan, and Chris; their spouses, Patrick, Joe, and Stacie; and to all my nieces and nephews—thank you for all the adventures over the years, the support through thick and thin. Hoping we all continue to achieve what others said can't be done. To the Byington, Hatcher, and Hills families, I'm forever grateful for your love and family bonds.

To my wise leadership guides, teachers, advisers, and friends who gave me the gift of their precious time and support in a pivotal "moment" in my career and life. I cannot thank you enough.

To Gary Heil. What can I say? You have been a most welcome provocateur, teacher, coach, muse, and friend. I could not have navigated this trek without you making me think more critically and calling me out when it mattered. I'll always remember our spirited debates, your wit, stories, wisdom, generosity, and the gift of your time. I am a huge fan of your podcast, *Leadership Lessons in the Fast Lane*, and your book, *Choose Love Not Fear: How the Best Leaders Build Cultures of Engagement and Innovation That Unleash Human Potential* (Heil, 2020). You make the world better by helping all of us see greater potential in ourselves. Thank you for continuing to push me to look for more questions and answers in places I didn't want to go or see or acknowledge or live in. It made me up my game. And, of course, made me a stronger advocate and a better mom.

To Nick Craig, your team at the Core Leadership Institute, and to my purpose family. I never realized how important purpose was to leading in life and business until I re-connected with it. The gifts of your wisdom, teaching, courage, and community are truly invaluable. The work may be hard but it's a game changer. You make the world a better place, businesses more successful, and all of our lives richer. *Leading from Purpose: Clarity and Confidence to Act When It Matters Most* (Craig, 2018) is a *must read.*

To Dana Born—visionary, mom, Ret. Brigadier General, woman of many firsts, Harvard professor, champion, ally, and mentor to so many. I cannot tell you how much your words of wisdom shifted my thinking and my journey. You made me realize that true leadership is about understanding yourself and the compass that guides you. Not only are you an incredible leader, but also an extraordinary mom and role model for future women leaders. Your humility, generosity, relatability, and authenticity make you the kind of incredible leader I'd follow anywhere. For helping me see more to leadership than just a book or a podcast, for helping me see the value of learning through our children's eyes, and for sharing the gifts of your daughters' leadership memories. It reminded me forever and always that our kids are watching.

A very special thanks to those who not only inspired us with their ideas and programs, but also with the gift of kindness, friendship and community.

To Melissa Kilby and Girl Up, and Carla Cuglietta, Tyler Waye, and YoungLeaders.World for offering inspiration and important lessons on leadership, building stronger communities, and being a positive voice. Thank you so much for the kindness and inspiration you gave to both me and Olivia. And to Sue Boardman, Abbie Hoffman, and the Gettysburg Foundation Executive Leadership Program, thank you for an incredible journey back in time on the battlefields of Gettysburg. It was an unforgettable adventure filled with leadership, culture, and life lessons that our family will never forget.

Thank you to those who inspired us to dream bigger—and to live our one wild and precious life.

To Amanda Doyle, Liz Book, and Together Rising, Diane Crump, Kyle Garman, Chris Koch, Judith A. Miller, Marcela Kirberger, Natalia Shehadeh, Rachel Bailey, Lauren Liess, Amy Knapp, Mindy Scheier, Dr. Bertrand Piccard, Scott Case, Lynn Haaland, Shannon Huffman Polson, Anne-Marie Slaughter, Leah JM Dean, Dr. Mitch Greene, Matthew Laney, Dr. Rachel Brem, Dan Linksey, Barbara

Bell, Jill Giffin, Katharine Manning, Stacy Middleman, Maria Abbe, Jess Galica, Emily Pereira, and my sisters in the Women's Bar Association Foundation.

Thank you to Chief, my Chief core group and sisters who have supported me in this journey.

A very special thanks to Beta reader extraordinaire Jamie Porter. Thank you to co-founders Carolyn Childers and Lindsay Kaplan for sharing your dream of pulling women executives together. It is so incredibly important and has been lacking for too long. A game-changing idea for sure!

To my book team who supported me through this publishing journey.

Eric Koester & the entire Creator Institute team, Brian Bies & the entire New Degree Press team, my fellow author Anjali Patel who talked me into writing a book, and to Bianca Myrtil, Tiffany Mosher, Lyn Solares, Simona Tirdova, Lauren Sweeney, Haley Newlin, Mackenzie Finklea. To the rest of this of this amazing team beyond the names here, I'm extremely grateful for your help and inspiration.

To my dear friends who have always had my back along this crazy ride of a career, who put up with my schedule, never being on time for anything, and my juggling act (although sometimes I was pretty good at it). My mom advisors and go-to problem solvers.

Lynn Michaels, Cynthia Alksne, Cecily Walsh, Lysa Senich, Gayla Keller, Lynell Shattls, Chris Corsac, Manon

MacGregor, Jody Partridge, Andra Davis, Tricia Haydon, Kirsten Adams, Kerri Harris.

A special thank you to Danny and Nicole Onorato, David and Lisa Schertler, and the entire crew at Schertler Onorato Mead & Sears, for your friendship and the unwavering support you have given me during an incredibly challenging time in my journey. I am still in awe of the work you do every day, the culture you have cultivated, and the skill, grit, brains, and compassion you bring to every case and every client. I've seen you in action, your masterful skill, and approach to hard cases, alongside your strong commitment to family and each other. I am truly honored to be part of your team.

Thank you to those who had a special impact on my career from my early years through today. I am forever grateful for your support, wisdom, and guidance over the years, and for believing in me along the way. I am especially grateful for the opportunity and gift of working with you. To those of you who called me out and warned me that warp speed was no way to live, I continue to be humbled (you know who you are).

Hon. Colleen Kollar-Kotelly, Fred Fielding, Jane Roberts, Susan Kerr, Steve Sokolow, Christina Corsac, Clara Rodriguez, Alice Fisher, Tiffany Moseley, Beatrice Seravello, Kyle Clark, Lystra Blake, Hon. Lee F. Satterfield, Linda Ramsburg, Patrick Conner, and the law school career counsellor whose name I no longer remember. And to Bill Gardner, Mark Srere, and Peter Buscemi, and each of your "better halves," Mindi, Jayne, and Judy, for making my early Big Law days quite the adventure! There are so many others to whom I am grateful in my career journey from law school jobs to my clerkship, my days as a prosecutor, and throughout Big Law. Too many to name in these pages. I will just say thank you again, humbly. I look forward to re-connecting in life.

Thank you to Hon. Eric H. Holder, Jr. for believing in me and for giving me the opportunity to serve in the job that will always be most near and dear to my heart. It was a great honor to serve as an Assistant US Attorney under your leadership.

To our family friends, our support network, and the gals and guys that kept the Hatcher family strong and moving in the right direction as we tried to navigate our crazy dual careers. I am forever grateful to you and your families for being part of ours.

Michele Brixius and her mom, sweet Arlene; Viviane Puffay and our "German" family, Mario, Alexa, and Sina Puffay; Jale Negel, Jessica Wohlgemuth, Tiemy Obara, Kimberley (Ramsburg) Rice, Adrien Cotton, Jason Knowles, Andre Crochet, Remy Rory, Shawn Gray, Michael Nicotra, Ann Bartlett, Ann, Bob and Abbie Henshaw, Jalene Spain Thomas, Coach Will, Allie Allen, Betsy Burke Parker, Wendy Powers.

Thank you to everyone in my "Author Community" who supported this book early on, several of whom were dedicated Beta readers who offered invaluable advice.

Kris Ullman, Cecily Walsh, Gina Locksley, Steven P. Sokolow, Jenny Bi, Anastasia Dzura, Jalene Thomas, Debra Salamon, Annie DeVito, Jennifer Asher, Jen Zipperer, Phyllis Ryan, Manny Alas, Jennifer Poersch, Shami Anand, Eric Koester, Kimberly O'Neil, Debra Curry, Laura Lawton Gee, Shannon McCracken, Anthony Alexia, Victoria Holstein, Kathleen McGovern, Lisa Manning, Maura Charles, Gillian Ward, Karen Silverman, Julie Bauer, Cynthia Steele, Keri Brown, Rachel Hess, Mary Ellen Kleiman, Stacey Kalamaras, Sharon Lebovitz Richmond, Daniel Aun, Denise Ricker, Cathy Cohen, Anjali Patel, Tara Tighe, Michelle Renaldo Ferguson, Glynna Christian, Nicholas Bonadies, Bridget Bailey Lipscomb, Jere Byington, Richard Orenstein, Kathleen Conway, Megan Romano, Richard Sibery, Greg Talbot, Tania Zamorsky, Carrie Collins, Christina Corsac, Rachel Tumidolsky Hardwick, Kate Lee, Mark McCullough, Diane Webb, Dante E. Daly, Elaine Altamar, Ann K. Batlle, Molly Cahill, Stacey Dash, Yiota Souras, Clara Rodriguez, Lynn Atkinson, K. L. Ligorner, Moira McCullough, Thomas Kelly, Gayla Keller, Natalia Sorgente, Steph Benecchi, Krista Tongring, Lilly Ann Sanchez, Schertler Onorato Mead & Sears LLP, Amy Verhulst, Rob Blume, Michele Gibbons, Kara Brockmeyer, Doug & Katie Coleman, Ellen Kollar, Jennifer Standig, Stacie Jeong, Jeannine Holt, Jennifer Daniels, Leslie Schrader, Kathleen Montgomery, Jenna Voss, Jennifer Cote, Michele Brixius, Marie H. Hills, Carin Carithers, Tiffany Moseley, Laura Gardner, Joseph Perry, Kaethe Carl, Karyn Smith, Chandra Branham, Mary-Beth Conway Donovan, Shayne Newell, Njoki Kamuiru, Adrien Cotton, Robin Cameron, Kyle Clark, Anna Romberg, Cynthia Alksne, Karyn Smith, Stephanie Craig, Kristen Podagiel, Jennifer Reichert.

My gratitude to Matt Mendelsohn for your incredible photography and Aida Colette for your ever-present magic in making one weary mom come to life!

To my amazing Italy crew for the best fiftieth birthday a girl could have and the trip of a lifetime. A way to live.

The Michaels, Puffays, Knudsons, O'Briens, Kellers, and Wrights.

And, last but not least . . .

To all the women warriors out there who gave me courage to speak out so that perhaps we might together change the world and unleash unlimited opportunities for all. This book is for you.

I did say a village, right? And so it goes . . . And so it grows.

Thank you to all who have touched my life in a special way.

Appendix

AUTHOR'S NOTE

Bell, Jacqueline. "Law360's Glass Ceiling Report: What You Need to Know." *Law360*, September 13, 2021. https://www.law360.com/articles/1418221/law360-s-glass-ceiling-report-what-you-need-to-know.

Conway-Hatcher, Amy. "Women Don't Need to Work Harder. The Legal Profession Needs to Evolve." *LinkedIn* (blog). July 20, 2021. https://www.linkedin.com/pulse/women-dont-need-work-harder-legal-profession-needs-amy-conway-hatcher/?trackingId=3YUD62llT-wS%2FS4t%2F8w7iyQ%3D%3D.

Huang, Jess, Irina Starikova, Delia Zanoschi, Alexis Krivkovich, and Lareina Yee. "Women in the Work Place 2020." *McKinsey & Company*, September 20, 2020. https://www.mckinsey.com/featured-insights/diversity-and-inclusion/women-in-the-workplace.

Sterling, Joyce, and Linda Chanow. "In Their Own Words: Experienced Women Lawyers Explain Why They Are Leaving

Their Law Firms and the Profession." *American Bar Association*, April 19, 2021. https://www.americanbar.org/content/dam/aba/administrative/women/intheirownwords-f-4-19-21-final.pdf.

CHAPTER ONE My Kitchen Meltdown

Huang, Jess, Irina Starikova, Delia Zanoschi, Alexis Krivkovich, and Lareina Yee. "Women in the Work Place 2020." *McKinsey & Company*, September 20, 2020. https://www.mckinsey.com/featured-insights/diversity-and-inclusion/women-in-the-workplace.

Meredith Corp. "3 Out of 4 Women Are Suffering from Burnout, According to New Harris Poll Commissioned by Meredith Corporation." *Meredith Corp.* news release, October 13, 2019. Meredith Corp. website. https://meredith.mediaroom.com/2019-10-03-American-Women-Confronting-Burnout-At-Epidemic-Levels-According-To-New-Harris-Poll-Commissioned-By-Meredith-Corporation, accessed October 21, 2021.

CHAPTER FIVE The Ruse

Bell, Jacqueline. "Law360's Glass Ceiling Report: What You Need to Know." *Law 360*, September 13, 2021. https://www.law360.com/articles/1418221/law360-s-glass-ceiling-report-what-you-need-to-know.

CHAPTER SEVEN The Frog in the Pot

Doyle, Glennon, and Amanda Doyle. "Sister Act: Who Is Amanda—and Seriously, How Does She Know All the

Things?" August 19, 2021. *We Can Do Hard Things with Glennon Doyle.* Podcast, 21:50-22:55. https://podcasts.apple.com/us/podcast/sister-act-who-is-amanda-and-seriously-how-does-she/id1564530722?i=1000532450192.

Doyle, Glennon, Amanda Doyle, and Abby Wambach. "Playing Our Roles: How Does Culture's Invention of Gender Typecast Every Last One of Us?" August 24, 2021. *We Can Do Hard Things with Glennon Doyle.* Podcast, 25:09. https://podcasts.apple.com/us/podcast/playing-our-roles-how-does-cultures-invention-of/id1564530722?i=1000532928102.

Reed, Ryan. "Watch Ruth Bader Ginsburg Talk Sexism, Equality in New Doc Trailer." *Rolling Stone,* March 27, 2018. https://www.rollingstone.com/movies/movie-news/watch-ruth-bader-ginsburg-talk-sexism-equality-in-new-doc-trailer-124574/.

CHAPTER EIGHT Big Law's Last Act

Blakely, Susan Smith. "Are Women Paying Enough Attention to Upward Mobility?" *ABA Journal,* June 29, 2021. https://www.abajournal.com/columns/article/are-women-lawyers-paying-enough-attention-to-upward-mobility.

Conway-Hatcher, Amy. "Women Don't Need to Work Harder. The Legal Profession Needs to Evolve." *LinkedIn* (blog). July 20, 2021. https://www.linkedin.com/pulse/women-dont-need-work-harder-legal-profession-needs-amy-conway-hatcher/?trackingId=3YUD62llT-wS%2FS4t%2F8w7iyQ%3D%3D.

CHAPTER ELEVEN Leveraging the Village

Sandberg, Sheryl. "Why We Have Too Few Women Leaders." Filmed December 2010. TEDWomen 2010 video, 14:42. https://www.ted.com/talks/sheryl_sandberg_why_we_have_too_few_women_leaders?language=en.

Sandberg, Sheryl. *Lean In: Women, Work, and the Will to Lead.* New York: Alfred A. Knopf, 2013.

Slaughter, Anne-Marie. "Why Women Still Can't Have It All." *The Atlantic*, August 16, 2012. https://www.theatlantic.com/magazine/archive/2012/07/why-women-still-cant-have-it-all/309020/.

Slaughter, Anne-Marie. *Unfinished Business: Women Men Work Family.* New York: Random House, 2015.

Yamada, Kobi. *What Do You Do With an Idea?* Seattle: Compendium, Inc., 2014.

CHAPTER TWELVE Game Changers

Chief. *Chief LinkedIn profile.* Accessed October 21, 2021. https://www.linkedin.com/company/joinchief/mycompany/.

Deutch, Gabby. "The Company Bringing Together Female Chief Executives." *JewishInsider,* June 2, 2021. https://jewishinsider.com/2021/06/chief-company-lindsay-kaplan/.

Together Rising. "Emergency Love Flash Mob for the Children." *Together Rising* (blog). May 29, 2018. https://togetherrising.org/emergency-love-flash-mob-for-the-children/.

von Tobel, Alexa. "How to Raise Venture Capital in a Hybrid World." *Fast Company,* October 8, 2021. https://www.fastcompany.com/90683996/how-to-raise-venture-capital-in-a-hybrid-world.

Made in the USA
Middletown, DE
20 January 2022

59215681R00146